LOW FAT
Chicken

LOW FAT
Chicken

Cosultant Editor
ANNE HILDYARD

southwater

This edition is published by Southwater

Southwater is an imprint of Anness Publishing Ltd
Hermes House, 88–89 Blackfriars Road, London SE1 8HA
tel. 020 7401 2077; fax 020 7633 9499
www.southwaterbooks.com; info@anness.com

© Anness Publishing Ltd 1997, 2001, 2006

UK agent: The Manning Partnership Ltd, 6 The Old Dairy,
Melcombe Road, Bath BA2 3LR; tel. 01225 478444; fax 01225 478440;
sales@manning-partnership.co.uk

UK distributor: Grantham Book Services Ltd, Isaac Newton Way,
Alma Park Industrial Estate, Grantham, Lincs NG31 9SD; tel. 01476 541080;
fax 01476 541061; orders@gbs.tbs-ltd.co.uk

North American agent/distributor: National Book Network,
4501 Forbes Boulevard, Suite 200, Lanham, MD 20706; tel. 301 459 3366;
fax 301 429 5746; www.nbnbooks.com

Australian agent/distributor: Pan Macmillan Australia, Level 18,
St Martins Tower, 31 Market St, Sydney, NSW 2000; tel. 1300 135 113;
fax 1300 135 103; customer.service@macmillan.com.au

New Zealand agent/distributor: David Bateman Ltd, 30 Tarndale Grove,
Off Bush Road, Albany, Auckland; tel. (09) 415 7664; fax (09) 415 8892

Publisher: Joanna Lorenz
Senior Cookery Editor: Linda Fraser
Project Editor: Anne Hildyard
Assistant Editor: Margaret Malone
Designer: Alan Marshall
Photographers: Karl Adamson, Edward Allwright, David Armstrong, James
Duncan, Michelle Garrett, Amanda Heywood, David Jordan and Peter Reilly
Recipes: Catherine Atkinson, Christine France, Shirley Gill, Shehzad Husain,
Sue Maggs, Liz Trigg and Steven Wheeler
Food for photography: Nicola Fowler, Jane Stevenson, Judy Williams
and Elizabeth Wolf-Cohen
Stylists: Madeleine Brehaut, Hilary Guy, Jo Harris and Blake Minton

For all recipes, quantities are given in both metric and imperial measures, and,
where appropriate, measures are also given in standard cups and spoons.
Follow one set, but not a mixture, because they are not interchangeable.

Previously published as *Step-by-Step: Low Fat Chicken*

1 3 5 7 9 10 8 6 4 2

CONTENTS

INTRODUCTION

Chicken is a popular food and rightly so. It is economical, quick to prepare and cook and it is endlessly versatile, adapting to any cooking method. It can be poached, stir-fried, roasted, crumbed and baked, casseroled and sautéed and combines well with just about any ingredient or flavour.

Although chicken has less fat and fewer calories than red meat, it is only low in fat when the skin is removed. Removing the skin lowers the fat by as much as 50 percent. Fortunately, cooking chicken with the skin, which adds flavour and retains moisture, then removing the skin before serving, will still give the reduced fat benefits.

Some of the recipes in *Step-by-Step Low Fat Chicken* have been cooked in their skin because of flavour retention or because the design of the recipe dictates that this is the best method. In these recipes, strip off the skin after cooking or before eating to minimize fat intake.

Cutting down on fat doesn't have to mean losing out on flavour, and there is no need to forego your favourite chicken dishes as the recipes in this book show. *Step-by-Step Low Fat Chicken* will help you make healthier choices of cooking methods that will ensure you enjoy chicken as much as ever.

Facts about Fats

It's important to know something about different fats before we can make changes to the way we eat – some fats are believed to be less harmful than others.

Fats in our foods are made up of building blocks of fatty acids and glycerol and their properties vary according to each combination. There are three main types of fatty acids; saturated, polyunsaturated and unsaturated or mono-unsaturated. There is always a combination of each of the three types in any food, but the amount of each type varies greatly from one food to another.

SATURATED FATS

All fatty acids are made up of chains of carbon atoms. Each atom has one or more free 'bonds' to link with other atoms and by doing so the fatty acid transports nutrients to cells throughout the body. Without these free 'bonds' the atom cannot form any links, that is to say, it's completely 'saturated'. Because of this, the body finds it hard to process the fatty acid into energy, so simply stores it as fat.

The main type of saturated fat is found in food of animal origin – meat and dairy products such as lard and butter, which are solid at room temperature. However, there are also some saturated fats of vegetable origin, notably coconut and palm oils. A few margarines and oils are processed by changing some of the unsaturated fatty acids to saturated ones; these are labelled 'hydrogenated vegetable oil' and should be avoided.

MONO-UNSATURATED FATS

These are found in foods such as olive oil, rapeseed oil, some nuts, oily fish and avocado pears. They may help lower the blood cholesterol and this could explain why in Mediterranean countries there is such a low incidence of heart disease.

Above: *Some oils, such as olive and rapeseed are thought to help lower blood cholesterol.*

Above left: *Animal products such as lard and butter and some margarines are major sources of saturated fats.*

POLYUNSATURATED FATS

There are two types, those of vegetable or plant origin, such as sunflower oil, soft margarine and seeds (omega 6) and those from oily fish (omega 3). Both are usually liquid at room temperature.

At one time it was believed to be beneficial to switch to polyunsaturates as they may also help lower cholesterol. Today most experts believe that it's more important to reduce the total intake of all kinds of fat.

Right: *Vegetable and plant oils and some margarines are high in polyunsaturated fat.*

The Cholesterol Question

Cholesterol is a fat-like substance which plays a vital role in the body. It's the material from which many essential hormones and vitamin D are made. However, too much saturated fat encourages the body to make more cholesterol than it needs or can get rid of.

Cholesterol is carried around the body, attached to proteins called high density lipoproteins (HDL), low density lipoproteins (LDL), and very low density lipoproteins (VLDL or triglycerides). After eating, the LDLs carry the fat in the blood to the cells where it's required. Any surplus should be excreted from the body; however, if there is too much LDL in the blood, some of the fat will be deposited on the walls of the arteries. This furring up gradually

narrows the arteries and is one of the most common causes of heart attacks and strokes. In contrast, HDLs appear to protect against heart disease. Whether high triglyceride levels are risk factors remains unknown.

For some people, an excess of cholesterol in the blood is a hereditary trait; in others, it's mainly due to the consumption of too much saturated fat. In both cases though, it can be reduced by a low fat diet. Many people believe

FATS & OILS		
Saturated	**Mono-unsaturated**	**Polyunsaturated**
Butter	Olive oil	Corn oil
Lard	Grapeseed oil	Safflower oil
Hard margarine	Rapeseed oil	Soya oil
Suet		Sunflower oil
Vegetarian suet		Walnut oil
Coconut oil		Soft margarines, labelled 'high in polyunsaturates'
Palm oil		

naturally high cholesterol foods such as egg yolks and offal should be avoided, but research has

shown that it is more important to reduce total fat intake.

Eating a Healthy Low Fat Diet

Eat a good variety of different foods every day to make sure you get all the nutrients you need.

1 Skimmed milk contains the same amount of calcium, protein and B vitamins as whole milk, but a fraction of the fat.
2 Natural low-fat yogurt, cottage cheese and fromage frais are all high in calcium and protein, and are good substitutes for cream.
3 Starchy foods such as rice, bread, potatoes, cereals and pasta should be eaten at every meal. These foods provide energy and some vitamins, minerals and dietary fibre.
4 Vegetables, salads and fruits should form a major part of the diet, and about 450 g/1 lb should be eaten each day.
5 Eat meat in moderation but eat plenty of fish, particularly oily fish such as mackerel, salmon, tuna, herring and sardines.

A few simple changes to a normal diet can reduce fat intake considerably. The following tips are designed to make the change to a healthier diet as easy as possible.

Meat and poultry
Red meats such as lamb, pork and beef are high in saturated fats, but chicken and turkey contain far less fat. Remove the skin before cooking and trim off any visible fat. Avoid sausages, burgers, patés, bacon and minced beef. Buy lean cuts of meat and skim any fat from the surface of stocks and stews.

Dairy products
Replace whole milk with skimmed or semi-skimmed and use low-fat yogurt, low-fat crème fraîche or fromage frais instead of cream. Eat cream, cream cheese and hard cheeses in moderation. There are reduced-fat cheeses on the market with 14% fat content which is half the fat content of full fat cheese. Use these wherever possible.

Spreads, oils and dressings
Use butter, margarine and low-fat spreads sparingly. Try to avoid using fat and oil for cooking. If you have to use oil, choose olive, corn, sunflower, soya, rapeseed and peanut oils, which are low in saturates. Look out for oil-free dressings and reduced fat mayonnaise.

Hidden fats
Biscuits, cakes, pastries, snacks and processed meals and curries all contain high proportions of fat. Get into the habit of reading food labels carefully and looking for a low-fat option.

Cooking methods
Grill, poach and steam foods whenever possible. If you do fry foods, use as little fat as possible and pat off the excess after browning, with kitchen paper. Make sauces and stews by first cooking the onions and garlic in a small quantity of stock, rather than frying in oil.

A selection of foods for a healthy low-fat diet.

EASY WAYS TO CUT DOWN FAT AND SATURATED FAT

EAT LESS	TRY INSTEAD
Butter and hard fats.	Try spreading butter more thinly, or replace it with a low fat spread or polyunsaturated margarine.
Fatty meats and high fat products such as pies and sausages.	Buy the leanest cuts of meat you can afford and choose low fat meats like skinless chicken or turkey. Look for reduced fat sausages and meat products. Eat fish more often, especially oily fish.
Full fat dairy products like cream, butter, hard margarine, milk and hard cheeses.	Choose skimmed or semi-skimmed milk and milk products, and try low fat yogurt, low fat fromage frais and lower fat cheeses such as skimmed milk soft cheese, reduced fat Cheddar, mozzarella or Brie.
Hard cooking fats such as lard or hard margarine.	Choose mono-unsaturated or polyunsaturated oils for cooking, such as olive, sunflower, corn or soya oil.
Rich salad dressings like mayonnaise or salad cream.	Make salad dressings with low fat yogurt or fromage frais, or use a healthy oil such as olive oil.
Fried foods.	Grill, microwave, steam or bake when possible. Roast meats on a rack. Fill up on starchy foods like pasta, rice and couscous. Choose jacket or boiled potatoes, not chips.
Added fat in cooking.	Use heavy-based or non-stick pans so you can cook with little or no added fat.
High fat snacks such as crisps, chocolate, cakes, pastries and biscuits.	Choose fresh or dried fruit, breadsticks or vegetable sticks. Make your own low fat cakes and bakes.

Choosing a Chicken

When choosing a fresh chicken, it should have a plump breast and the skin should be creamy in colour. The tip of the breast bone should be pliable.

A bird's dressed weight is taken after plucking and drawing and may include the giblets (neck, gizzard, heart and liver). A frozen chicken must be thawed slowly in the refrigerator or a cool room. Never put it in hot water, as this will toughen the flesh.

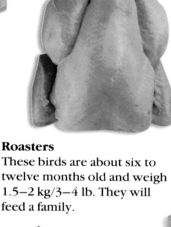

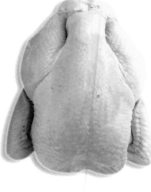

Roasters
These birds are about six to twelve months old and weigh 1.5–2 kg/3–4 lb. They will feed a family.

Boilers
These are about twelve months and over and weigh between 2–3 kg/4–6 lb. They require long, slow cooking, around 2–3 hours, to make them tender.

Spring chickens
These birds are about three months old and weigh 900 g– 1.25 kg/2–2½ lb. They will serve three to four people.

Cornfed chickens
These are free-range birds, and are generally more expensive. They usually weigh 1.25– 1.5 kg/2½–3 lb.

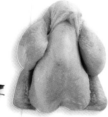

Double poussins
These are eight to ten weeks old and weigh 800–900 g/ 1¾–2 lb. They will serve two people. Poussins are best roasted, grilled or pot-roasted.

Poussins
These are four to six weeks old and weigh 450 g–550 g/ 1–1¼ lb. They are enough for one person.

12

Cuts of Chicken

Today, chicken is available pre-packaged in a variety of different ways. If you do not want to buy a whole bird, you can choose from the many selected cuts on the market. Most cooking methods are suitable for all cuts, but some are especially suited to specific cuts of meat.

Leg
This comprises the thigh and drumstick. Large pieces with bones, such as this, are suitable for slow-cooking, such as casseroling or poaching.

Skinless boneless thigh
This makes tasks such as stuffing and rolling much quicker, as it is already skinned and jointed.

Liver
This makes a wonderful addition to pâtés or to salads.

Drumstick
The drumstick is a firm favourite for barbecuing or frying, either in batter or rolled in breadcrumbs.

Wing
The wing does not supply much meat, and is often barbecued or fried.

Ground chicken
This is not as strongly flavoured as, say, ground beef, but may be used as a substitute in some recipes.

Breast
This comprises tender white meat and can be simply cooked in butter, as well as stuffed.

Thigh
The thigh is suitable for casseroling and other slow-cooking methods.

Tips for Reducing Fat

• Keep chicken meat tender by roasting with the skin on. Remove the skin before serving, for reduced fat benefits.

• Use a cooking method that needs little or no fat such as poaching, grilling, stir-frying, baking or roasting.

• Instead of making traditional gravy, skim off all the fat from the roasting tin and make a low fat gravy with the meat juices, herbs and chicken stock.

• When roasting chicken, add garlic to the roasting tin with the chicken, then purée the roasted garlic with the juices in the tin to make a tasty sauce without fat.

• Remove all the skin and any visible fat from chicken thighs, drumsticks and breasts before cooking (right).

REDUCE THE FAT, NOT THE FLAVOUR

• Add flavour with chopped garlic, fresh herbs and spices to skinned chicken before cooking. Rub the chosen flavour into the chicken.

• Add a bouquet garni to stews or casseroles, if possible make it with a mixture of fresh herbs and tie them together with string, or use commercial bags of bouquet garni.

• Marinate in wine, cider, vinegar, lemon or lime juice. Skin and slash chicken joints, then pour over the marinade.

• Sprinkle finely chopped shallots, onions or spring onions over the chicken, or if the chicken is whole, place a small whole onion in the cavity before cooking. Remove before serving.

• Before cooking, spread chicken breasts with prepared mustard to add a piquant flavour.

• Serve plainly cooked chicken with a fruit or vegetable salsa. Make the salsa from any selection of finely chopped fruit or vegetables. Spring onions and chopped fresh herbs such as coriander or parsley add fresh flavour.

Low Fat Cooking Methods

• Oven bake chicken with vegetables and herbs in paper parcels.

• Grilling – marinate first to add flavour. Fat drips off chicken during cooking.

• Steaming – this retains the moisture and needs no added fat. Add flavour boosters such as lemon rind, garlic and herbs, or steam over smoky-flavoured tea.

• Baking – dip chicken breasts in egg white then in a light coating of rolled oats to produce tender chicken.

• Stir-fry in a small amount of hot oil in a wok – the oil spreads further when hot, meaning that less is needed and the chicken is then quickly sealed and doesn't absorb much.

• Poaching – poach skinless chicken pieces in stock with vegetables, then blend the cooked vegetables to make a delicious purée to serve with the chicken.

Chicken Roulades

These chicken rolls make a light lunch dish for two, or a starter for four. They can be sliced and served cold with a salad.

NUTRITIONAL NOTES
PER PORTION:

ENERGY 239 Kcals/1008 KJ **FAT** 14.5 g
SATURATED FAT 4.6 g
CHOLESTEROL 56.2 mg

Makes 4

INGREDIENTS
4 boned and skinned chicken thighs
115 g/4 oz chopped frozen spinach
15 g/½ oz/1 tbsp butter
25 g/1 oz/2 tbsp pine nuts
pinch of ground nutmeg
25 g/1 oz/7 tbsp fresh white
    breadcrumbs
4 rashers rindless streaky bacon
30 ml/2 tbsp olive oil
150 ml/¼ pint/⅔ cup white wine
    or chicken stock
10 ml/2 tsp cornflour
30 ml/2 tbsp single cream
15 ml/1 tbsp chopped fresh chives
salt and freshly ground black pepper

breadcrumbs

streaky bacon

spinach

butter

pine nuts

chives

olive oil

single cream

cornflour

chicken thighs

1 Preheat the oven to 180°C/350°F/ Gas 4. Place the chicken thighs between clear film and flatten with a rolling pin.

2 Put the spinach and butter into a saucepan, heat gently until the spinach has defrosted, then increase the heat and cook rapidly, stirring occasionally until all the moisture has been driven off. Add the pine nuts, seasoning, nutmeg and fresh breadcrumbs.

3 Divide the filling between the chicken pieces and roll up neatly. Wrap a rasher of bacon around each piece and secure with string.

4 Heat the oil in a large frying pan and brown the rolls all over. Drain through a slotted spoon and place in a shallow ovenproof dish.

5 Pour over the wine or stock, cover, and bake for 15–20 minutes, or until tender. Transfer the chicken to a serving plate and remove the string. Strain the cooking liquid into a saucepan.

6 Mix the cornflour to a smooth paste with a little cold water and add to the juices in the pan, along with the cream. Bring to the boil to thicken, stirring all the time. Adjust the seasoning and add the chives. Pour the sauce round the chicken and serve.

Spiced Chicken Livers

Chicken livers can be bought frozen, but make sure that you defrost them thoroughly before using. Serve as a first course or light meal along with a mixed salad and garlic bread.

Serves 4

INGREDIENTS
350 g/12 oz chicken livers
115 g/4 oz/1 cup plain flour
2.5 ml/½ tsp ground coriander
2.5 ml/½ tsp ground cumin
2.5 ml/½ tsp ground cardamom seeds
1.25 ml/¼ tsp ground paprika
1.25 ml/¼ tsp ground nutmeg
90 ml/6 tbsp olive oil
salt and freshly ground black pepper
garlic bread, to serve

chicken livers

olive oil

flour

coriander

cardamom seeds

cumin

paprika

nutmeg

1 Dry the chicken livers on paper towels, removing any unwanted pieces. Cut the large livers in half and leave the smaller ones whole.

2 Mix the flour with all the spices and the seasoning.

NUTRITIONAL NOTES
PER PORTION:

ENERGY 297 Kcals/1248 KJ FAT 14.4 g
SATURATED FAT 2.9 g
CHOLESTEROL 332.5 mg

3 Coat the first batch of livers with spiced flour, separating each piece. Heat the oil in a large frying pan and fry the livers in small batches. (This helps to keep the oil temperature high and prevents the flour from becoming soggy.)

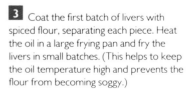

4 Fry quickly, stirring frequently, until crispy. Keep warm and repeat with the remaining livers. Serve immediately with warm garlic bread.

Chicken Tikka

The red food colouring gives this dish its traditional bright colour. Serve with lemon wedges and a crisp mixed salad.

Serves 4

INGREDIENTS

1 × 1.75 kg/3½ lb chicken
mixed salad leaves, e.g. frisée and
 oakleaf lettuce or radicchio,
 to serve

FOR THE MARINADE
150 ml/¼ pint/⅔ cup plain low fat
 yogurt
5 ml/1 tsp ground paprika
10 ml/2 tsp grated fresh root ginger
1 garlic clove, crushed
10 ml/2 tsp garam masala
2.5 ml/½ tsp salt
red food colouring (optional)
juice of 1 lemon

lemon

chicken

salt

yogurt

paprika

ginger

garlic

garam masala

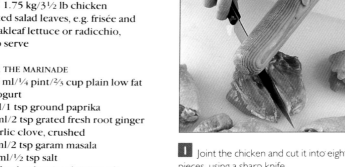

1 Joint the chicken and cut it into eight pieces, using a sharp knife.

2 Mix all the marinade ingredients in a large dish, add the chicken pieces to coat and chill for 4 hours or overnight to allow the flavours to penetrate the flesh.

NUTRITIONAL NOTES
PER PORTION:
ENERGY 131 Kcals/554 KJ   FAT 4.5 g
SATURATED FAT 1.4 g
CHOLESTEROL 55.4 mg

3 Preheat the oven to 200°C/400°F/ Gas 6. Remove the chicken pieces from the marinade and arrange them in a single layer in a large ovenproof dish. Bake for 30–40 minutes or until tender.

4 Baste with a little of the marinade while cooking. Arrange on a bed of salad leaves and serve hot or cold.

Cornfed Chicken Salad

A light first course for eight people or a substantial main course for four. Arrange attractively on individual plates to serve.

Serves 8

INGREDIENTS

1 × 1.75 kg/3½ lb cornfed chicken
300 ml/½ pint/1¼ cups white wine
   and water, mixed
24 × 5 mm/¼ in slices French bread
1 garlic clove, peeled
225 g/8 oz French beans
115 g/4 oz fresh young spinach leaves
2 sticks celery, thinly sliced
2 spring onions, thinly sliced
2 sun-dried tomatoes, chopped
fresh chives and parsley, to garnish

FOR THE VINAIGRETTE

30 ml/2 tbsp red wine vinegar
90 ml/6 tbsp olive oil
15 ml/1 tbsp wholegrain mustard
15 ml/1 tbsp runny honey
30 ml/2 tbsp chopped mixed fresh
   herbs, e.g. thyme, parsley and chives
10 ml/2 tsp finely chopped capers
salt and freshly ground black pepper

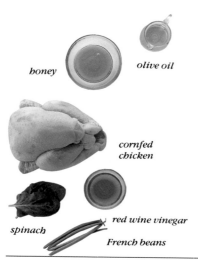

honey

olive oil

cornfed chicken

spinach

red wine vinegar

French beans

1 Preheat the oven to 190°C/375°F/ Gas 5. Put the chicken into a casserole with the wine and water. Roast for 1½ hours until tender. Leave to cool in the liquid. Remove the skin and bones and cut the flesh into small pieces.

2 To make the vinaigrette, put all the ingredients into a screw-topped jar and shake vigorously to emulsify. Adjust the seasoning to taste.

3 Toast the French bread under the grill or in the oven until dry and golden brown, then lightly rub with the peeled garlic clove.

4 Trim the French beans, cut into 5 cm/ 2 in lengths and cook in boiling water until just tender (*al dente*). Drain and rinse under cold running water.

5 Wash the spinach, remove the stalks and tear into small pieces. Arrange on serving plates with the sliced celery, French beans, sun-dried tomatoes, chicken and spring onions.

NUTRITIONAL NOTES

PER PORTION:

ENERGY 306 Kcals/1285 KJ **FAT** 9.9 g
SATURATED FAT 2.3 g
CHOLESTEROL 54.9 mg

6 Spoon over the vinaigrette dressing. Arrange the toasted croûtes on top, garnish with extra fresh chives and parsley, if desired, and serve immediately.

Sesame Seed Chicken Bites

Best served warm, these crunchy bites are delicious accompanied by a glass of chilled dry white wine.

Makes 20

INGREDIENTS
175 g/6 oz raw chicken breast
2 cloves garlic, crushed
2.5 cm/1 in piece root ginger, peeled and grated
1 × size 4 egg white
5 ml/1 tsp cornflour
25 g/1 oz/¼ cup shelled pistachios, roughly chopped
60 ml/4 tbsp sesame seeds
30 ml/2 tbsp grapeseed oil
salt and freshly ground black pepper

FOR THE SAUCE
45 ml/3 tbsp/¼ cup hoisin sauce
15 ml/1 tbsp sweet chilli sauce

TO GARNISH
root ginger, finely shredded
pistachios, roughly chopped
fresh dill sprigs

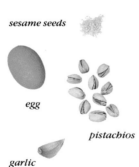

sesame seeds

egg

pistachios

garlic

ginger

1 Place the chicken, garlic, grated ginger, egg white and cornflour into the food processor and process them to a smooth paste.

2 Stir in the pistachios and season well with salt and pepper.

NUTRITIONAL NOTES
PER PORTION:

ENERGY 53 Kcals/223 KJ **FAT** 4.1 g
SATURATED FAT 0.6 g
CHOLESTEROL 3.8 mg

3 Roll into 20 balls and coat with sesame seeds. Heat the wok and add the oil. When the oil is hot, stir-fry the chicken bites in batches, turning regularly until golden. Drain on kitchen towels.

4 Make the sauce by mixing together the hoisin and chilli sauces in a bowl. Garnish the bites with shredded ginger, pistachios and dill, then serve hot, with a dish of sauce for dipping.

Tandoori Chicken

Traditionally baked in a clay oven called a tandoor, this tasty dish can also be cooked in a conventional oven.

Serves 4

INGREDIENTS
4 chicken quarters
175 ml/6 fl oz/³⁄₄ cup low fat
  natural yogurt
5 ml/1 tsp garam masala
5 ml/1 tsp grated fresh root ginger
1 garlic clove, crushed
7.5 ml/1½ tsp chilli powder
1.5 ml/¼ tsp ground turmeric
5 ml/1 tsp ground coriander
15 ml/1 tbsp lemon juice
5 ml/1 tsp salt
few drops of red food colouring
30 ml/2 tbsp corn oil

FOR THE GARNISH
mixed salad leaves
lime wedges

chicken

natural
yogurt

garam
masala

ginger
root

garlic

chilli
powder

turmeric

ground
coriander

corn oil

lemon
juice

1 Skin the chicken quarters, rinse them under cold water and pat them dry with kitchen paper. Make 2 slits into the flesh of each piece, place the pieces in a shallow dish and set aside.

2 Mix the yogurt, garam masala, ginger, garlic, chilli powder, turmeric, ground coriander, lemon juice, salt, red colouring and oil in a bowl. Beat so that all the ingredients are well mixed together.

3 Cover the chicken quarters with the spice mixture and leave to marinate for about 3 hours.

4 Preheat the oven to 240°C/475°F/ Gas 9. Transfer the chicken pieces to an ovenproof dish.

5 Bake for 20–25 minutes or until the chicken is cooked right through and browned on top.

6 Remove the dish from the oven, transfer the chicken pieces to a serving dish and garnish with the salad leaves and lime wedges.

NUTRITIONAL NOTES
Per portion:

ENERGY 242 Kcals/1018 KJ **FAT** 10.6 g
SATURATED FAT 2.7 g
CHOLESTEROL 81.9 mg

Italian Vegetable Soup

The success of this clear soup depends on the quality of the stock, so use home-made vegetable stock rather than stock cubes.

Serves 4

INGREDIENTS
1 small carrot
1 baby leek
1 celery stick
50 g/2 oz green cabbage
900 ml/1 ½ pints/3¾ cups
    vegetable stock
1 bay leaf
115 g/4 oz/1 cup cooked cannellini
    beans
25 g/1 oz/⅕ cup soup pasta, such as
    tiny shells, bows, stars or elbows
salt and freshly ground black pepper
snipped fresh chives, to garnish

stock

cabbage

bay leaf

chives

baby leek

celery

carrot

pasta

1 Cut the carrot, leek and celery into 5 cm/2 in long julienne strips. Slice the cabbage very finely.

2 Put the stock and bay leaf into a large saucepan and bring to the boil. Add the carrot, leek and celery, cover and simmer for 6 minutes.

NUTRITIONAL NOTES
PER PORTION:
ENERGY 126 Kcals/529 KJ **FAT** 2.2 g
SATURATED FAT 0.6 g
CHOLESTEROL 19 mg

3 Add the cabbage, beans and pasta shapes. Stir, then simmer uncovered for a further 4-5 minutes, or until the vegetables and pasta are tender.

4 Remove the bay leaf and season to taste. Ladle into four soup bowls and garnish with snipped chives. Serve immediately.

Sweetcorn and Chicken Soup

This popular classic Chinese soup is very easy to make.

NUTRITIONAL NOTES

PER PORTION:

ENERGY 163 Kcals/686 KJ **FAT** 4.6 g
SATURATED FAT 1.1 g
CHOLESTEROL 72.4 mg

Serves 4-6

INGREDIENTS
1 chicken breast fillet, about
    115 g/4 oz, cubed
10 ml/2 tsp light soy sauce
15 ml/1 tbsp Chinese rice wine
5 ml/1 tsp cornflour
60 ml/4 tbsp cold water
5 ml/1 tsp sesame oil
30 ml/2 tbsp groundnut oil
5 ml/1 tsp grated fresh root
    ginger
1 litre/1¾ pints/4 cups chicken
    stock
425 g/15 oz can cream-style
    sweetcorn
225 g/8 oz can sweetcorn kernels
2 eggs, beaten
2–3 spring onions, green parts
    only, cut into tiny rounds
salt and ground black pepper

cornflour

chicken stock

cream-style sweetcorn

chicken

sweetcorn kernels

Chinese rice wine

egg

sesame oil

ginger

1 Mince the chicken in a food processor, taking care not to over-process. Transfer the chicken to a bowl and stir in the soy sauce, rice wine, cornflour, water, sesame oil and seasoning. Cover and leave for about 15 minutes to absorb the flavours.

2 Heat a wok over a medium heat. Add the groundnut oil and swirl it around. Add the ginger and stir-fry for a few seconds. Add the stock, creamed sweetcorn and sweetcorn kernels. Bring to just below boiling point.

3 Spoon about 90 ml/6 tbsp of the hot liquid into the chicken mixture until it forms a smooth paste and stir. Return to the wok. Slowly bring to the boil, stirring constantly, then simmer for 2–3 minutes until cooked.

4 Pour the beaten eggs into the soup in a slow steady stream, using a fork or chopsticks to stir the top of the soup in a figure-of-eight pattern. The egg should set in lacy shreds. Serve immediately with the spring onions sprinkled over.

Warm Chicken Salad with Shallots and Mangetouts

Succulent cooked chicken pieces are combined with vegetables in a light chilli dressing.

Serves 6

INGREDIENTS

50 g/2 oz mixed salad leaves
50 g/2 oz baby spinach leaves
50 g/2 oz watercress
30 ml/2 tbsp chilli sauce
30 ml/2 tbsp dry sherry
15 ml/1 tbsp light soy sauce
15 ml/1 tbsp tomato ketchup
10 ml/2 tsp olive oil
8 shallots, finely chopped
1 garlic clove, crushed
350 g/12 oz skinless, boneless
   chicken breast, cut into thin strips
1 red pepper, seeded and sliced
175 g/6 oz mangetouts, trimmed
400 g/14 oz can baby sweet corn,
   drained and halved
275 g/10 oz can brown rice
salt and ground black pepper
parsley sprig, to garnish

1 Arrange the mixed salad leaves, tearing up any large ones, and the spinach leaves on a serving dish. Add the watercress and toss to mix.

2 In a small bowl, mix together the chilli sauce, sherry, soy sauce and tomato ketchup and set aside.

mixed salad leaves   *spinach*   *watercress*   *chilli sauce*   *dry sherry*

light soy sauce   *tomato ketchup*   *olive oil*   *shallots*   *garlic*

chicken breasts   *red pepper*   *mange-touts*   *baby sweetcorn*   *brown rice*

3 Heat the oil in a large non-stick frying pan or wok. Add the shallots and garlic and stir-fry over medium heat for 1 minute.

4 Add the chicken and stir-fry for 3–4 minutes.

NUTRITIONAL NOTES

PER PORTION:

ENERGY 184 Kcals/774 KJ **FAT** 3.9 g
SATURATED FAT 0.9 g
CHOLESTEROL 25.1 mg

COOK'S TIP
Use other lean meat such as turkey breast, beef or pork in place of the chicken.

5 Add the pepper, mangetout, sweetcorn and rice and stir-fry for 2–3 minutes.

6 Pour in the chilli sauce mixture and stir-fry for 2–3 minutes, until hot and bubbling. Season to taste. Spoon the chicken mixture over the salad leaves, toss together to mix and serve immediately, garnished with fresh parsley.

Curried Chicken Salad

Serves 4

INGREDIENTS

2 cooked chicken breasts, boned
175 g/6 oz French beans
350 g/12 oz multi-coloured penne
150 ml/¹/₄ pint/²/₃ cup low-fat yogurt
5 ml/1 tsp mild curry powder
1 garlic clove, crushed
1 green chilli, seeded and
 finely chopped
30 ml/2 tbsp chopped
 fresh coriander
4 firm ripe tomatoes, skinned,
 seeded and cut in strips
salt and ground black pepper
coriander leaves, to garnish

multi-coloured penne

chicken breasts

French beans

green chilli

coriander

low-fat yogurt

tomatoes

garlic

1 Remove the skin from the chicken and cut in strips. Cut the green beans in 2.5 cm/1 in lengths and cook in boiling water for 5 minutes. Drain and rinse under cold water.

2 Cook the pasta in a large pan of boiling, salted water until *al dente*. Drain and rinse thoroughly.

NUTRITIONAL NOTES

PER PORTION:

ENERGY 449 Kcals/1884 KJ FAT 5.1 g
SATURATED FAT 1.3 g
CHOLESTEROL 38 mg

3 To make the sauce, mix the yogurt, curry powder, garlic, chilli and chopped coriander together in a bowl. Stir in the chicken pieces and leave to stand for 30 minutes.

4 Transfer the pasta to a glass bowl and toss with the beans and tomatoes. Spoon over the chicken and sauce. Garnish with coriander leaves.

Chicken and Pasta Salad

This is a delicious way to use up left-over cooked chicken, and makes a filling meal.

Serves 4

INGREDIENTS
225 g/8 oz tri-coloured
    pasta twists
30 ml/2 tbsp bottled pesto sauce
15 ml/1 tbsp olive oil
1 beefsteak tomato
12 stoned black olives
225 g/8 oz cooked French beans
350 g/12 oz cooked chicken, cubed
salt and freshly ground black pepper
fresh basil, to garnish

tomato

pesto sauce

French beans

basil

olive oil

pasta twists

chicken

black olives

1 Cook the pasta in plenty of boiling, salted water until *al dente* (about 12 minutes or as directed on the packet).

2 Drain the pasta and rinse in plenty of cold running water. Put into a bowl and stir in the pesto sauce and olive oil.

NUTRITIONAL NOTES
PER PORTION:

ENERGY 416 Kcals/1745 KJ FAT 13.9 g
SATURATED FAT 3.1 g
CHOLESTEROL 67.9 mg

3 Skin the tomato by placing in boiling water for about 10 seconds and then into cold water, to loosen the skin.

4 Cut the tomato into small cubes and add to the pasta with the olives, seasoning and French beans cut into 4 cm/1 ½ in lengths. Add the cubed chicken. Toss gently together and transfer to a serving platter. Garnish with fresh basil.

Spicy Chicken Salad

Serves 6

INGREDIENTS

5 ml/1 tsp ground cumin seeds
5 ml/1 tsp ground paprika
5 ml/1 tsp ground turmeric
1–2 garlic cloves, crushed
30 ml/2 tbsp lime juice
4 chicken breasts, boned
    and skinned
225 g/8 oz rigatoni
1 red pepper, seeded and chopped
2 sticks celery, sliced thinly
1 shallot or small onion,
    finely chopped
25 g/1 oz stuffed green
    olives, halved
30 ml/2 tbsp runny honey
15 ml/1 tbsp wholegrain mustard
15–30 ml/1–2 tbsp lime juice
salt and ground black pepper
mixed salad leaves, to serve

honey

chicken breasts

cumin seeds

onion

red pepper

lime

turmeric *garlic*

celery

mixed salad leaves

rigatoni

stuffed olives

paprika

1 Mix the cumin, paprika, turmeric, garlic, seasoning and lime juice in a bowl. Rub this mixture over the chicken breasts. Lay in a shallow dish, cover with clear film and leave in a cool place for about 3 hours or overnight.

2 Preheat the oven to 200°C/400°F/ Gas 6. Put the chicken on a grill rack in a single layer and bake for 20 minutes. (Or grill for 8–10 minutes on each side.)

3 Cook the rigatoni in a large pan of boiling, salted water until *al dente*. Drain and rinse under cold water. Leave to drain thoroughly.

4 Put the red pepper, celery, shallot or small onion and olives into a large bowl with the pasta.

5 Mix the honey, mustard and lime juice together in a bowl and pour over the pasta. Toss to coat.

6 Cut the chicken in bite-size pieces. Arrange the mixed salad leaves on a serving dish, spoon the pasta mixture in the centre and top with the spicy chicken pieces.

NUTRITIONAL NOTES
PER PORTION:

ENERGY 277 Kcals/1165 KJ **FAT** 5.6 g
SATURATED FAT 1.4 g
CHOLESTEROL 49 mg

Dijon Chicken Salad

An attractive and elegant dish to serve for lunch
with herb and garlic bread.

Serves 4

INGREDIENTS
4 boned and skinned chicken breasts
mixed salad leaves, e.g. frisée and
   oakleaf lettuce or radicchio,
   to serve

FOR THE MARINADE
30 ml/2 tbsp Dijon mustard
3 garlic cloves, crushed
15 ml/1 tbsp grated onion
60 ml/4 tbsp white wine

FOR THE MUSTARD DRESSING
30 ml/2 tbsp tarragon wine vinegar
5 ml/1 tsp Dijon mustard
5 ml/1 tsp clear honey
90 ml/6 tbsp olive oil
salt and freshly ground black pepper

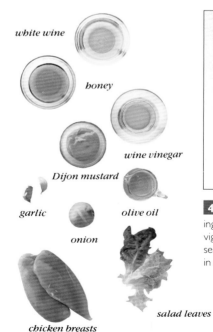

white wine

honey

wine vinegar

Dijon mustard

garlic

onion

olive oil

salad leaves

chicken breasts

1 Mix all the marinade ingredients together in a shallow glass or earthenware dish that is large enough to hold the chicken in a single layer.

2 Turn the chicken over in the marinade to coat completely, cover with clear film and then chill in the refrigerator overnight.

3 Preheat the oven to 190°C/375°F/Gas 5. Transfer the chicken and the marinade into an ovenproof dish, cover with foil and bake for about 35 minutes or until tender. Leave to cool in the liquid.

4 Put all the mustard dressing ingredients into a screw-topped jar, shake vigorously to emulsify, and adjust the seasoning. (This can be made several days in advance and stored in the refrigerator.)

5 Slice the chicken thinly, fan out the slices and arrange on a serving dish with the salad leaves.

6 Spoon over some of the mustard dressing and serve.

NUTRITIONAL NOTES
PER PORTION:

ENERGY 125 Kcals/527 KJ **FAT** 6.5 g
SATURATED FAT 1.2 g
CHOLESTEROL 26.9 mg

Warm Stir-fried Salad

Warm salads are becoming increasingly popular because they are delicious and nutritious. Arrange the salad leaves on four individual plates, so the hot stir-fry can be served quickly on to them, ensuring the lettuce remains crisp and the chicken warm.

NUTRITIONAL NOTES
PER PORTION:

ENERGY 219 Kcals/920 KJ **FAT** 7.4 g
SATURATED FAT 1.6 g
CHOLESTEROL 48.4 mg

Serves 4

INGREDIENTS
15 ml/1 tbsp fresh tarragon
2 boneless, skinless chicken breasts,
   about 225 g/8 oz each
5 cm/2 in piece root ginger, peeled
   and finely chopped
45 ml/3 tbsp light soy sauce
15 ml/1 tbsp sugar
15 ml/1 tbsp sunflower oil
1 Chinese lettuce
½ frisée lettuce, torn into
   bite-size pieces
115 g/4 oz/cup unsalted cashews
2 large carrots, peeled and cut into
   fine strips
salt and freshly ground black pepper

chicken breast

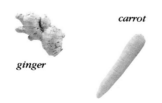

carrot

ginger

cashews

1 Chop the tarragon.

2 Cut the chicken into fine strips and place in a bowl.

3 To make the marinade, mix together in a bowl the tarragon, ginger, soy sauce, sugar and seasoning.

4 Pour the marinade over the chicken strips and leave for 2–4 hours.

5 Strain the chicken from the marinade. Heat the wok, then add the oil. When the oil is hot, stir-fry the chicken for 3 minutes, add the marinade and bubble for 2–3 minutes.

6 Slice the Chinese lettuce and arrange on a plate with the frisée. Toss the cashews and carrots together with the chicken, pile on top of the bed of lettuce and serve immediately.

Grilled Chicken Salad with Lavender and Sweet Herbs

Lavender may seem like an odd salad ingredient, but its delightful scent has a natural affinity with sweet garlic, orange and other wild herbs. A serving of corn meal polenta makes this salad both filling and delicious.

Serves 4

INGREDIENTS
4 boneless chicken breasts
850 ml/1½ pints/3¾ cups light
  chicken stock
175 g/6 oz/1 cup fine polenta or corn
  meal
50 g/2 oz butter
450 g/1 lb young spinach
175 g/6 oz lamb's lettuce
8 sprigs fresh lavender
8 small tomatoes, halved
salt and black pepper

LAVENDER MARINADE
6 fresh lavender flowers
10 ml/2 tsp finely grated orange zest
2 cloves garlic, crushed
10 ml/2 tsp clear honey
salt
30 ml/2 tbsp olive oil, French or
  Italian
10 ml/2 tsp chopped fresh thyme
10 ml/2 tsp chopped fresh marjoram

1 To make the marinade, strip the lavender flowers from the stems and combine with the orange zest, garlic, honey and salt. Add the olive oil and herbs. Slash the chicken deeply, spread the mixture over the chicken and leave to marinate in a cool place for at least 20 minutes.

polenta

spinach

orange

garlic

thyme

lavender   *chicken breasts*

2 To make the polenta, bring the chicken stock to the boil in a heavy saucepan. Add the corn meal in a steady stream, stirring all the time until thick: this will take 2–3 minutes. Turn the cooked polenta out on to a 2.5-cm/1-in-deep buttered tray and allow to cool.

3 Heat the grill (broiler) to a moderate temperature. (If using a barbecue, let the embers settle to a steady glow.) Grill (broil) the chicken for about 15 minutes, turning once.

4 Cut the polenta into 2.5 cm/1 in cubes with a wet knife. Heat the butter in a large frying-pan (skillet) and fry the polenta until golden.

COOK'S TIP

Lavender marinade is a delicious flavouring for salt-water fish as well as chicken. Try it over grilled cod, haddock, halibut, sea bass and bream.

NUTRITIONAL NOTES
PER PORTION:

ENERGY 352 Kcals/1479 KJ **FAT** 9.4 g
SATURATED FAT 2.1 g
CHOLESTEROL 43.3 mg

5 Wash the salad leaves and spin dry, then divide between 4 large plates. Slice each chicken breast and lay over the salad. Place the polenta among the salad, decorate with sprigs of lavender and tomatoes, season and serve.

QUICK CHICKEN DISHES

Lemon Chicken Stir-fry

It is essential to prepare all the ingredients before
you begin so they are ready to cook. This dish is cooked
in minutes.

Serves 4

INGREDIENTS
4 boned and skinned chicken breasts
15 ml/1 tbsp light soy sauce
75 ml/5 tbsp cornflour
1 bunch spring onions
1 lemon
1 garlic clove, crushed
15 ml/1 tbsp caster sugar
30 ml/2 tbsp sherry
150 ml/¼ pint/⅔ cup chicken stock
60 ml/4 tbsp olive oil
salt and freshly ground black pepper

NUTRITIONAL NOTES
PER PORTION:
ENERGY 298 Kcals/1249 KJ FAT 9.9 g
SATURATED FAT 2.13 g
CHOLESTEROL 53.8 mg

1 Divide the chicken breasts into two natural fillets. Place each between two sheets of clear film and flatten to a thickness of 5 mm/¼ in with a rolling pin.

2 Cut into 2.5 cm/1 in strips across the grain of the fillets. Put the chicken into a bowl with the soy sauce and toss to coat. Sprinkle over 60 ml/4 tbsp cornflour to coat each piece.

3 Trim the roots off the spring onions and cut diagonally into 1 cm/½ in pieces. With a swivel peeler, remove the lemon rind in thin strips and cut into fine shreds, or, if in a hurry, grate finely. Reserve the lemon juice. Have ready the garlic, sugar, sherry, stock, lemon juice and remaining cornflour blended to a paste with water.

caster sugar
garlic
olive oil
spring onions
lemon
soy sauce
cornflour
chicken breasts

4 Heat the oil in a wok or large frying pan and cook the chicken very quickly in small batches for 3–4 minutes until lightly coloured. Remove and keep warm while frying the rest of the chicken.

5 Add the spring onions and garlic to the pan and cook for 2 minutes.

6 Add the remaining ingredients and bring to the boil, stirring until thickened. Add more sherry or stock if necessary and stir until the chicken is evenly covered with sauce. Reheat for 2 more minutes. Serve immediately.

Chicken Teriyaki

A bowl of boiled rice is the ideal accompaniment to this Japanese-style chicken dish.

Serves 4

INGREDIENTS
450 g/1 lb boneless, skinless
    chicken breasts
orange segments and mustard and
    cress, to garnish

FOR THE MARINADE
5 ml/1 tsp sugar
15 ml/1 tbsp rice wine
15 ml/1 tbsp dry sherry
30 ml/2 tbsp dark soy sauce
rind of 1 orange, grated

orange

rice wine

soy sauce

chicken breast

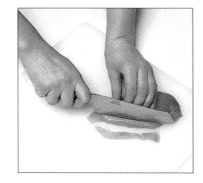

1 Finely slice the chicken.

2 Mix all the marinade ingredients together in a bowl.

COOK'S TIP
Make sure the marinade is brought to the boil and cooked for 4–5 minutes, because it has been in contact with raw chicken.

3 Place the chicken in a bowl, pour over the marinade and leave to marinate for 15 minutes.

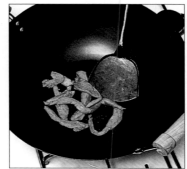

4 Heat the wok, add the chicken and marinade and stir-fry for 4–5 minutes. Serve garnished with orange segments and mustard and cress.

Chicken with Olives

If you use a non-stick pan you can cook these chicken escalopes in the minimum of oil.

Serves 4

INGREDIENTS
4 boned and skinned
  chicken breasts
1.5 ml/¼ tsp cayenne pepper
15–30 ml/1–2 tbsp extra virgin
  olive oil
1 garlic clove, finely chopped
16–24 stoned black olives
6 ripe plum tomatoes, chopped
small handful of fresh basil leaves

plum tomatoes

chicken

cayenne pepper

garlic

olive oil

stoned black olives

1 Carefully remove the fillets (the long finger-shaped muscle on the back of each breast) and reserve for another use.

2 Place each chicken breast between two sheets of clear film and flatten with a rolling pin to a thickness of about 1 cm/ ½ in. Season with the cayenne.

3 Heat 15 ml/1 tbsp of the olive oil in a non-stick frying pan over a high heat. Add the chicken and sear on both sides. Lower the heat and cook for 4–5 minutes until golden brown and just tender, turning them once. Using tongs, transfer the chicken to warmed serving plates. Keep hot while you cook the tomatoes and olives.

4 Reheat the oil in the pan (adding a little more if necessary) and fry the garlic for 1 minute until golden. Stir in the olives, cook for another minute. Stir in the tomatoes. Shred the basil and add to the olive and tomato mixture, spoon the sauce over the chicken and serve.

NUTRITIONAL NOTES
PER PORTION:

ENERGY 204 Kcals/859 KJ **FAT** 8.5 g
SATURATED FAT 1.9 g
CHOLESTEROL 53.7 mg

Chicken with Cashews

This hot and spicy Indian dish has a deliciously thick and nutty sauce, and is best served with plenty of plain boiled rice.

Serves 6

INGREDIENTS

2 onions
30 ml/2 tbsp tomato purée
50 g/2 oz/½ cup cashew nuts
7.5 ml/1½ tsp garam masala
1 garlic clove, crushed
5 ml/1 tsp chilli powder
15 ml/1 tbsp lemon juice
1.5 ml/¼ tsp ground turmeric
5 ml/1 tsp salt
15 ml/1 tbsp low fat natural yogurt
15 ml/1 tbsp corn oil
15 ml/1 tbsp chopped fresh
  coriander, plus extra to garnish
15 ml/1 tbsp sultanas
450 g/1 lb boned and skinned
  chicken breasts, cubed
175 g/6 oz/1½ cups button
  mushrooms, halved
300 ml/½ pint/1¼ cups water

onion

garam masala

garlic

casbew nuts

chicken

*button
mushrooms*

chilli powder

turmeric

corn oil

sultanas

lemon juice

natural yogurt

*fresh
coriander*

1 Cut the onions into quarters and place in a food processor or blender. Process for about 1 minute.

2 Add the tomato purée, cashews, garam masala, garlic, chilli powder, lemon juice, turmeric, salt and yogurt to the onions. Process for 1–1½ minutes more.

3 Heat the oil in a saucepan and fry the spice mixture over a medium heat for about 2 minutes, lowering the heat if necessary.

4 Add the coriander, sultanas and chicken and stir-fry for 1 minute more.

5 Add the mushrooms, pour in the water and bring to a simmer. Cover the pan and cook over a low heat for about 10 minutes.

6 After this time, check that the chicken is cooked through and the sauce is thick. Cook for a little longer if necessary. Garnish with chopped fresh coriander and serve.

NUTRITIONAL NOTES

PER PORTION:

ENERGY 187 Kcals/784 KJ **FAT** 9.8 g
SATURATED FAT 1.9 g
CHOLESTEROL 43.2 mg

PUZZLED? PUZZLED? PUZZLED?

ARROWORD

Enter your answers as indicated by the arrows, including items connected with our TV star, then read the letters in the shaded squares to spell a cricketer he played a cariacature of in a series of adverts (1,1,5). Answers on facing page.

Grid clues and answers:

Clue	Answer
Our star's surname	
Remove to safety	
Part of a candle	W I C K
Region	A R E A
Honey-making insect	B
Fish that's often tinned	
Supper	T E A
Took advantage of	U S E D
Female sheep	
After that	T H E N
Hawaiian wreath	L E I
Bird's limb	W I N G
E.g. parsley or thyme	
Archaic word meaning 'before'	E R E
Cloth scrap	R A G
Musical show starring Lea Michele	
Was taught	L E A R
Time period	E R A
Produce from chickens	E G G S
Chewing substance, often mint flavoured	G U M
Our star's first name	
Not liquid or solid	G A S
Our star's role in the Inbetweeners, Mr ___	E

TV

Solve our crossword, then rearrange the letters in the shaded squares to reveal the name of a TV series (5,5,3)

ACROSS

1 Claymation children's show featuring a penguin (5)
6 The ___ US drama which starred Dominic West and Idris Elba (4)
8 Channel 5's Alex Polizzi is ___ Inspector (3,5)
10 See 22 Across
11 Wayne ___ dancer who has appeared on reality shows including Come Dine With Me (5)
12 Actress who plays Emmerdale's Megan Macey, ___ Faye (6)
15 ___ Maxwell Martin, star of Poppy Shakespeare (4)
16 Hollyoaks student played by Laurie Duncan, ___ Kane (6)
17 ___ Geller, Friends character who was played by David Schwimmer (4)
19 The surname of Home And Away father and daughter Alf and Roo (7)

DOWN

2 American ___ US talent series (4)
3 New Channel drama starri
4 One of

ALPHAPUZZLE™

Alphapuzzle™ tests your logic and word power. Each grid number represents a letter. Every letter of the alphabet is used. Use the given letter or letters – below the main grid – to start. **Solution on Monday.**

DIFFICULTY: 6/10; TARGET: 20 mins; **CLUE:** Fix; so be it, Donald!

YESTERDAY'S SOLUTION: Across: Surreal, Dart, Hewn, Laxative, Strong, Refute, Metier (clue), Police, Unbiased, Play, Scan, Unnerve.
Down: Aspect, Eunuch, Wren, Opinion, Jetlag, Risque, Elixir, Pedant, Dutiful, Perk, Cravat, Crazed.

(Clues)

1 ...derful purse design (5)

...njoying a pickle in Greece (9)

3 Mean Dan to organise talk on personal details (4,3,7)

4 Virginia considered train an alternative (7)

5 Betting on a line about a dog (7)

7 One outwardly fat landowner (5)

8 Viewer pursues glorious duck (9)

9 Agreement only on fat old piece (8,6)

14 Arrived with rope and right capturing device (9)

16 Officer in prison has a dire problem (9)

18 Stroll when tea runs out (7)

19 Working under ship in strip (7)

22 Dorothy holds record at warehouse (5)

24 Track money after school (5)

...r tsar,

...5)
...s lid

...ff, but he's not

...ad about port (9)
...at's round, as it
...s (5)
...ct class (5)
...wisely spars nude in the subway (9)

25 Notes suggest a down payment (7)

26 Working to get dessert, we hear, in the bathroom (2,5)

27 Ceremony sounds correct (4)

28 Peer to see star actor roaming round island (10)

WEDNESDAY'S SOLUTION

ACROSS: 1 Disband, 5 Rummage, 9 Homestead, 10 Later, 11 Impress, 12 Radical, 13 Once upon a time, 18 Sleight of hand, 20 Related, 23 Plunger, 25 Least, 26 Eliminate, 27 Yielded, 28 Greatly.

DOWN: 1 Dahlia, 2 Semaphore, 3 Aisle, 4 Dress suit 5 Rider, 6 Melodrama, 7 Attic, 8 Enrolled,

Chicken in Spicy Yogurt

Plan this dish well in advance; the extra-long marinating time is necessary to develop a really mellow spicy flavour.

NUTRITIONAL NOTES
PER PORTION:
ENERGY 158 Kcals/663 KJ FAT 5.1 g
SATURATED FAT 1.6 g
CHOLESTEROL 58 mg

Serves 6

INGREDIENTS
6 chicken pieces
juice of 1 lemon
5 ml/1 tsp salt

FOR THE MARINADE
5 ml/1 tsp coriander seeds
10 ml/2 tsp cumin seeds
6 cloves
2 bay leaves
1 onion, quartered
2 garlic cloves
5 cm/2 in piece root ginger,
    peeled and roughly chopped
2.5 ml/^{1}/$_2$ tsp chilli powder
5 ml/1 tsp turmeric
150 ml/^{1}/$_4$ pint/^{2}/$_3$ cup natural
    yogurt
lemon, lime or coriander, to
    garnish

lemon

yogurt

coriander seeds

root ginger

onion

garlic

bay leaves

chilli powder

turmeric

cumin seeds

cloves

1 Skin the chicken joints and make deep slashes in the fleshiest parts with a sharp knife. Sprinkle over the lemon and salt and rub in.

2 Spread the coriander and cumin seeds, cloves and bay leaves in the bottom of a large frying pan and dry-fry over a moderate heat until the bay leaves are crispy.

3 Cool the spices and grind coarsely with a pestle and mortar.

4 Finely mince the onion, garlic and ginger in a food processor or blender. Add the ground spices, chilli, turmeric and yogurt, then strain in the lemon juice from the chicken.

5 Arrange the chicken in a single layer in a roasting tin. Pour over the marinade, then cover and chill for 24–36 hours.

6 Occasionally turn the chicken pieces in the marinade. Preheat the oven to 200°C/400°F/Gas 6. Cook the chicken for 45 minutes. Serve hot or cold, garnished with fresh leaves and slices of lemon or lime.

Spicy Chicken with Mint

For this tasty dish, the chicken is first boiled before being quickly stir-fried in a little oil, to ensure that it is cooked through.

Serves 4

INGREDIENTS
275 g/10 oz boned and skinned
   chicken breast, cut into strips
300 ml/½ pint/1¼ cups water
15 ml/1 tbsp corn oil
2 small bunches of spring onions,
   roughly chopped
10 ml/2 tsps chopped fresh
   root ginger
5 ml/1 tsp crumbled dried red chilli
30 ml/2 tbsp lemon juice
15 ml/1 tbsp chopped
   fresh coriander
15 ml/1 tbsp chopped fresh mint
3 tomatoes, seeded and
   roughly chopped
5 ml/1 tsp salt
mint and coriander sprigs,
   to garnish

chicken

spring onions

corn oil

fresh ginger

lemon juice

fresh coriander

tomatoes

fresh mint

NUTRITIONAL NOTES
PER PORTION:
ENERGY 155 Kcals/649 KJ **FAT** 8.2 g
SATURATED FAT 1.6 g
CHOLESTEROL 30.4 mg

1 Put the chicken and water into a saucepan, bring to the boil and lower the heat to medium. Cook for about 10 minutes or until the water has evaporated and the chicken is tender. Remove from the heat and set aside.

2 Heat the oil in a large non-stick frying pan or shallow saucepan and stir-fry the spring onions for about 2 minutes until soft.

3 Drain the cooked chicken strips and add them to the pan. Stir-fry for about 3 minutes over a medium heat.

4 Gradually add the ginger, dried chilli, lemon juice, fresh coriander and mint, tomatoes and salt. Toss over the heat to warm the tomatoes through and allow the flavours to blend. Transfer to a serving dish and garnish with the fresh mint and coriander sprigs.

Fragrant Chicken Curry

In this dish, the mildly spiced sauce is thickened using lentils rather than the traditional onions fried in ghee.

Serves 4

INGREDIENTS

75 g/3 oz/½ cup red lentils
30 ml/2 tbsp mild curry powder
10 ml/2 tsp ground coriander
5 ml/1 tsp cumin seeds
475 ml/16 fl oz/2 cups vegetable stock
8 chicken thighs, skinned
225 g/8 oz fresh shredded, or frozen
  spinach, thawed and well drained
15 ml/1 tbsp chopped fresh coriander
salt and freshly ground black pepper
sprigs of fresh coriander, to garnish
white or brown basmati rice and
  grilled poppadums, to serve

fresh coriander

spinach

cumin seeds

curry powder

ground coriander

lentils

chicken thigh

NUTRITIONAL NOTES
Per portion:

ENERGY 232 Kcals/975 KJ FAT 7.5 g
SATURATED FAT 1.9 g
CHOLESTEROL 73 mg

1 Rinse the lentils under cold running water. Put into a large, heavy-based saucepan with the curry powder, ground coriander, cumin seeds and stock.

2 Bring to the boil then lower the heat. Cover and gently simmer for 10 minutes.

3 Add the chicken and spinach. Re-cover and simmer gently for a further 40 minutes, or until the chicken has cooked.

4 Stir in the chopped coriander and season to taste. Serve garnished with fresh coriander and accompanied by the rice and grilled poppadums.

Grilled Chicken with Pica de Gallo Salsa

This dish originates from Mexico. Its hot fruity flavours form the essence of Tex-Mex Cooking.

NUTRITIONAL NOTES
Per portion:
ENERGY 197 Kcals/826 KJ FAT 7.1 g
SATURATED FAT 1.7 g
CHOLESTEROL 53.8 mg

Serves 4

INGREDIENTS
4 chicken breasts
pinch of celery salt and cayenne
    pepper combined
30 ml/2 tbsp vegetable oil
corn chips, to serve

FOR THE SALSA
275 g/10 oz watermelon
175 g/6 oz canteloupe melon
1 small red onion
1–2 green chillies
30 ml/2 tbsp lime juice
60 ml/4 tbsp chopped fresh coriander
pinch of salt

1 Preheat a moderate grill. Slash the chicken breasts deeply to speed up the cooking time.

2 Season the chicken with celery salt and cayenne, brush with oil and grill for about 15 minutes.

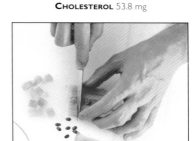

3 To make the salsa, remove the rind and as many seeds as you can from the melons. Finely dice the flesh and put it into a bowl.

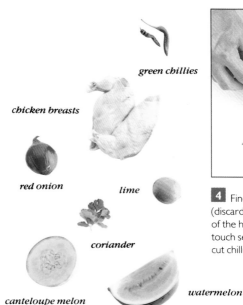

green chillies

chicken breasts

red onion

lime

coriander

canteloupe melon

watermelon

4 Finely chop the onion, split the chillies (discarding the seeds which contain most of the heat) and chop. Take care not to touch sensitive skin areas when handling cut chillies. Mix with the melon.

5 Add the lime juice and chopped coriander, and season with a pinch of salt. Turn the salsa into a small bowl.

6 Arrange the grilled chicken on a plate and serve with the salsa and a handful of corn chips.

Chicken Liver Stir-fry

The final sprinkling of lemon, parsley and garlic gives this dish a delightful fresh flavour and wonderful aroma.

Serves 4

INGREDIENTS
500 g/1 ¼ lb chicken livers
75 g/3 oz/6 tbsp butter
175 g/6 oz field mushrooms
50 g/2 oz chanterelle mushrooms
3 cloves garlic, finely chopped
2 shallots, finely chopped
150 ml/¼ pint/⅔ cup medium sherry
3 fresh rosemary sprigs
30 ml/2 tbsp fresh parsley, chopped
rind of 1 lemon, grated
salt and freshly ground pepper
fresh rosemary sprigs, to garnish
4 thick slices of white toast, to serve

1 Clean and trim the chicken livers to remove any gristle or muscle.

2 Season the livers generously with salt and freshly ground black pepper, tossing well to coat thoroughly.

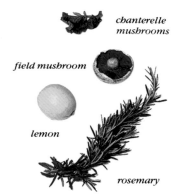

chanterelle mushrooms

field mushroom

lemon

rosemary

3 Heat the wok and add 15 g/½ oz/ 1 tbsp of the butter. When melted, add the livers in batches (melting more butter where necessary but reserving 25 g/1 oz/ 2 tbsp for the vegetables) and flash-fry until golden brown. Drain with a slotted spoon and transfer to a plate, then place in a low oven to keep warm.

4 Cut the field mushrooms into thick slices and, depending on the size of the chanterelles, cut in half.

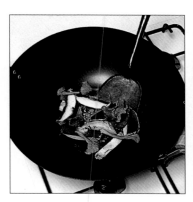

5 Heat the wok and add the remaining butter. When melted, stir in two-thirds of the chopped garlic and the shallots and stir-fry for 1 minute until golden brown. Stir in the mushrooms and continue to cook for a further 2 minutes.

NUTRITIONAL NOTES
PER PORTION:

ENERGY 277 Kcals/1163 KJ **FAT** 13.7 g
SATURATED FAT 3.2 g
CHOLESTEROL 475 mg

6 Add the sherry, bring to the boil and simmer for 2–3 minutes until syrupy. Add the rosemary, salt and pepper and return livers to the pan. Stir-fry for 1 minute. Garnish with extra sprigs of rosemary, and serve sprinkled with a mixture of lemon, parsley and the remaining chopped garlic, with slices of toast.

Chicken and Bean Bake

A delicious combination of chicken, fresh tarragon and mixed beans, topped with a layer of tender potatoes, ideal served with broccoli florets and baby carrots for a filling family meal.

Serves 6

INGREDIENTS

900 g/2 lb potatoes
50 g/2 oz/½ cup reduced-fat mature
 Cheddar cheese, finely grated
600 ml/1 pint/2½ cups skimmed
 milk, plus 30–45 ml/2–3 tbsp
 skimmed milk
30 ml/2 tbsp chopped fresh chives
2 leeks, washed and sliced
1 onion, sliced
30 ml/2 tbsp dry white wine
40 g/1½ oz/3 tbsp half-fat spread
40 g/1½ oz/¼ cup plain
 wholemeal flour
300 ml/½ pint/1¼ cups chicken
 stock, cooled
350 g/12 oz cooked skinless
 chicken breast, diced
225 g/8 oz/3 cups brown cap
 mushrooms, sliced
300 g/11 oz can red kidney beans
400 g/14 oz can flageolet beans
400 g/14 oz can black-eyed beans
30–45 ml/2–3 tbsp chopped
 fresh tarragon
salt and ground black pepper

potatoes

reduced-fat mature Cheddar cheese

skimmed milk

fresh chives

leeks

onion

cooked chicken breasts

dry white wine

half-fat spread

plain wholemeal flour

chicken stock

red kidney beans

flageolet beans

black-eyed beans

brown cap mushrooms

fresh tarragon

1 Preheat the oven to 200°C/400°F/ Gas 6. Cut the potatoes into chunks and cook in lightly salted, boiling water for 15–20 minutes, until tender. Drain thoroughly and mash. Add the cheese, 30–45 ml/2–3 tbsp milk and chives, season to taste and mix well. Keep warm and set aside.

2 Meanwhile, put the leeks and onion in a saucepan with the wine. Cover and cook gently for 10 minutes, until the vegetables are just tender, stirring occasionally.

3 In the meantime, put the half-fat spread, flour, remaining milk and stock in a saucepan. Heat gently, whisking continuously, until the sauce comes to the boil and thickens. Simmer gently for 3 minutes, stirring.

4 Remove the pan from the heat and add the leek mixture, chicken and mushrooms and mix well.

5 Add all the drained beans to the sauce and stir in with the tarragon and seasoning. Heat gently until the chicken mixture is piping hot, stirring.

COOK'S TIP

Sweet potatoes in place of standard potatoes work just as well in this recipe, and turkey or lean ham can be used in place of the chicken for a change.

6 Transfer it to an ovenproof dish and spoon or pipe the potato mixture over the top, to cover the chicken mixture completely. Bake for about 30 minutes, until the potato topping is crisp and golden brown. Serve immediately.

NUTRITIONAL NOTES
PER PORTION:

ENERGY 445 Kcals/1871 KJ **FAT** 8.9 g
SATURATED FAT 1.9 g
CHOLESTEROL 50.4 mg

Tuscan Chicken

This simple peasant casserole has all the flavours of traditional Italian ingredients.

Serves 4

INGREDIENTS
5 ml/1 tsp olive oil
8 skinned chicken thighs
1 onion, thinly sliced
2 red peppers, seeded and sliced
1 garlic clove, crushed
300 ml/½ pint/1¼ cups passata
150 ml/¼ pint/⅔ cup dry white wine
1 large fresh oregano sprig, or
  5 ml/1 tsp dried oregano
400 g/14 oz can cannellini
  beans, drained
45 ml/3 tbsp fresh white
  breadcrumbs
salt and ground black pepper

chicken thighs

olive oil

red pepper

onion

sprig oregano

fresh breadcrumbs

dry white wine

cannellini beans

garlic

NUTRITIONAL NOTES
PER PORTION:

ENERGY 248 Kcals/1045 KJ **FAT** 7.5 g
SATURATED FAT 2.1 g
CHOLESTEROL 73 mg

1 Heat the oil in a non-stick frying pan and fry the chicken until golden brown. Remove with a slotted spoon and keep hot. Add the onion and peppers to the pan and sauté gently until softened, but not brown. Stir in the garlic.

2 Add the chicken, passata, white wine and oregano. Season well, then bring to the boil with the lid on.

3 Lower the heat and simmer gently, without a lid, for 30–35 minutes or until the chicken is tender and cooked through. Stir occasionally.

4 Stir in the cannellini beans and simmer for 5 minutes more to heat through. Sprinkle evenly with the breadcrumbs and flash under a hot grill until golden brown.

Oat-crusted Chicken with Sage

Oats make a good coating for savoury foods and sealing in the natural juices means that you do not need to add extra fat.

Serves 4

INGREDIENTS

45 ml/3 tbsp skimmed milk
10 ml/2 tsp mustard powder
40 g/1½ oz/½ cup rolled oats
45 ml/3 tbsp chopped sage leaves
8 skinned chicken thighs or drumsticks
120 ml/4 fl oz/½ cup low fat fromage frais
5 ml/1 tsp wholegrain mustard
salt and ground black pepper
fresh sage leaves, to garnish

skimmed milk

mustard powder

rolled oats

sage leaves

chicken thighs

fromage frais

wholegrain mustard

1 Preheat the oven to 200°C/400°F/Gas 6. Mix the milk and mustard powder in a cup. Mix the oats with 30 ml/2 tbsp of the sage in a shallow dish. Add salt and pepper to taste. Brush the chicken with the mustard and milk mixture and press into the oats to coat evenly.

2 Place the chicken on a baking sheet and bake for about 40 minutes, or until the juices run clear, not pink, when pierced through the thickest part.

3 Meanwhile, mix the low fat fromage frais, mustard and remaining sage. Season to taste. Garnish the chicken with fresh sage and serve hot or cold, with the sauce.

COOK'S TIP
If fresh sage is not available, choose another fresh herb such as thyme or parsley, instead of using a dried alternative.

NUTRITIONAL NOTES
Per portion:

ENERGY 214 Kcals/898 KJ **FAT** 6.6 g
SATURATED FAT 1.8 g
CHOLESTEROL 64.6 mg

Country Chicken Casserole

Succulent chicken joints in a vegetable sauce are
excellent served with brown rice or pasta.

NUTRITIONAL NOTES

PER PORTION:

ENERGY 377 Kcals/1585 KJ **FAT** 11.7 g
SATURATED FAT 2.9 g
CHOLESTEROL 76.1 mg

Serves 4

INGREDIENTS

2 chicken breasts, skinned
2 chicken legs, skinned
30 ml/2 tbsp plain wholemeal flour
15 ml/1 tbsp sunflower oil
300 ml/½ pint/1¼ cups chicken stock
300 ml/½ pint/1¼ cups white wine
30 ml/2 tbsp passata
15 ml/1 tbsp tomato purée
4 rashers lean smoked back bacon
1 large onion, sliced
1 garlic clove, crushed
1 green pepper, seeded and sliced
225 g/8 oz/3 cups button
   mushrooms
225 g/8 oz carrots, sliced
1 bouquet garni
225 g/8 oz frozen Brussels sprouts
175 g/6 oz/1½ cups frozen
   petit pois
salt and ground black pepper
chopped fresh parsley, to garnish

1 Preheat the oven to 180°C/350°F/
Gas 4. Coat the chicken joints with
seasoned flour.

2 Heat the oil in a large flameproof
casserole, add the chicken and cook
until browned all over. Remove the
chicken using a slotted spoon and
keep warm.

3 Add any remaining flour to the pan
and cook for 1 minute. Gradually stir
in the stock and wine, then add the
passata and tomato purée.

*chicken breasts
and legs*

*plain
wholemeal
flour*

*sunflower
oil*

*chicken
stock*

*dry
white
wine*

passata

*tomato
purée*

*smoked back
bacon*

onion

garlic

*green
pepper*

*button
mushrooms*

carrots

*bouquet
garni*

*Brussels
sprouts*

petit pois

4 Bring to the boil, stirring continuously, then add the chicken, bacon, onion,
garlic, pepper, mushrooms, carrots and bouquet garni and stir. Cover and bake for
1½ hours, stirring once or twice.

COOK'S TIP
Use fresh Brussels sprouts and peas if available, and use red wine in place of white for a change.

5 Stir in the Brussels sprouts and petit pois, re-cover and bake for a further 30 minutes.

6 Remove and discard the bouquet garni. Add seasoning to the casserole, garnish with chopped fresh parsley and serve immediately.

Chicken and Apricot Filo Pie

Filo is the low fat cook's best friend, as it contains little fat and needs only a light brushing of melted butter to create a crisp crust.

Serves 6

INGREDIENTS
75 g/3 oz/½ cup bulgur wheat
120 ml/4 fl oz/½ cup boiling water
30 ml/2 tbsp butter
1 onion, chopped
450 g/1 lb lean minced chicken
50 g/2 oz/¼ cup ready-to-eat dried
  apricots, finely chopped
25 g/1 oz/¼ cup blanched
  almonds, chopped
5 ml/1 tsp ground cinnamon
2.5 ml/½ tsp ground allspice
60 ml/4 tbsp low fat fromage frais
15 ml/1 tbsp snipped fresh chives
30 ml/2 tbsp chopped fresh parsley
10 large sheets of filo pastry
salt and ground black pepper
chives, to garnish

bulgur wheat

onion

minced chicken

fromage frais

ground allspice

chives

dried apricots

filo pastry

ground cinnamon

NUTRITIONAL NOTES
Per portion:

ENERGY 239 Kcals/1004 KJ FAT 6.3 g
SATURATED FAT 1.6 g
CHOLESTEROL 43.0 mg

1 Preheat the oven to 200°C/400°F/ Gas 6. Put the bulgur wheat in a bowl and add the boiling water. Leave to soak for 5–10 minutes, until all the water is absorbed.

2 Heat 15 ml/1 tbsp of the butter in a non-stick pan, and gently fry the onion and chicken until pale golden.

3 Stir in the apricots, almonds and bulgur. Cook for 2 minutes more. Remove from the heat and stir in the cinnamon, allspice, fromage frais, fresh chives and parsley. Season to taste with salt and pepper.

4 Melt the remaining butter. Cut the filo pastry into 25 cm/10 in rounds. Cover the pastry rounds with a cloth.

5 Line a 23 cm/9 in loose-based flan tin with three of the pastry rounds, brushing each one lightly with butter as you layer them. Spoon in the chicken mixture, then cover with three more rounds, brushed with butter as before.

6 Crumple the remaining rounds and place them on top of the pie, then brush with melted butter. Bake for about 30 minutes, until golden brown and crisp. Serve the pie hot or cold, cut in wedges and garnished with chives.

Crispy Spring Chickens

These small birds are about 900 g/2 lb to 1.25 kg/
2½ lb in weight and are delicious either hot or cold.

Serves 4

INGREDIENTS
2 × 900 g/2 lb chickens
salt and freshly ground black pepper

FOR THE HONEY GLAZE
30 ml/2 tbsp clear honey
30 ml/2 tbsp sherry
15 ml/1 tbsp vinegar

sherry

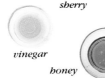

vinegar

honey

chicken

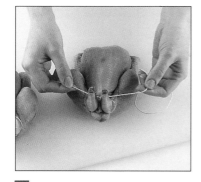

1 Preheat the oven to 180°C/350°F/
Gas 4. Tie the birds into a neat shape and
place on a wire rack over the sink. Pour
over boiling water to plump the flesh and
pat dry with paper towels.

2 Mix the honey, sherry and vinegar
together and brush over the birds. Season
with salt and pepper.

NUTRITIONAL NOTES
PER PORTION:

ENERGY 135 Kcals/565 KJ FAT 4.3 g
SATURATED FAT 1.4 g
CHOLESTEROL 56.3 mg

3 Place the rack into a roasting tin and
bake the birds for 45–55 minutes. Baste
well with the honey glaze until crisp and
golden brown.

Chicken in Herb Crusts

The chicken breasts can be brushed with melted butter instead of mustard before being coated in the bread-crumb mixture. Serve with new potatoes and salad.

Serves 4

INGREDIENTS
4 boned and skinned chicken breasts
15 ml/1 tbsp Dijon mustard
30 ml/2 tbsp chopped fresh parsley
50 g/2 oz/1 cup fresh breadcrumbs
15 ml/1 tbsp dried mixed herbs
25 g/1 oz/2 tbsp butter, melted
salt and freshly ground black pepper

parsley

breadcrumbs

Dijon mustard

chicken breasts

dried herbs

1 Preheat the oven to 180°C/350°F/ Gas 4. Lay the chicken breasts in a greased ovenproof dish and spread with the mustard. Season with salt and freshly ground black pepper.

2 Mix the breadcrumbs and herbs together thoroughly.

3 Press onto the chicken to coat. Spoon over the melted butter. Bake uncovered for 20 minutes or until tender and crisp.

NUTRITIONAL NOTES
PER PORTION:

ENERGY 217 Kcals/915 KJ **FAT** 7.9 g
SATURATED FAT 1.9 g
CHOLESTEROL 54.0 mg

Chicken Bobotie

Perfect for a buffet party, this mild curry dish is set with savoury custard, which makes serving easy. Serve with boiled rice and chutney.

NUTRITIONAL NOTES
Per portion:

ENERGY 334 Kcals/1403 KJ FAT 12.8 g
SATURATED FAT 3.1 g
CHOLESTEROL 138 mg

Serves 8

INGREDIENTS
two thick slices white bread
450 ml/¾ pint/1⅞ cups milk
30 ml/2 tbsp olive oil
2 medium onions, finely chopped
40 ml/2½ tbsp medium curry powder
1.25 kg/2½ lb minced raw chicken
15 ml/1 tbsp apricot jam, chutney or
   caster sugar
30 ml/2 tbsp wine vinegar or lemon
   juice
3 large eggs, beaten
50 g/2 oz/⅓ cup raisins or sultanas
12 whole almonds
salt and freshly ground black pepper

minced chicken

raisins

apricot jam

lemon

onion

olive oil

egg

almonds

bread

curry powder

1 Preheat the oven to 180°C/350°F/ Gas 4. Soak the bread in 150 ml/¼ pint/ ⅔ cup of the milk. Heat the oil in a frying pan and gently fry the onions until tender then add the curry powder and cook for a further 2 minutes.

2 Add the minced chicken and brown all over, separating the grains of meat as they brown. Remove from the heat, season with salt and freshly ground black pepper, add the apricot jam, chutney or caster sugar and vinegar or lemon juice.

3 Mash the bread in the milk and add to the pan together with one of the beaten eggs and the raisins.

4 Grease a 1.5 litre/2½ pint shallow ovenproof dish with butter. Spoon in the chicken mixture and level the top. Cover with buttered foil and bake for 30 minutes.

5 Meanwhile, beat the remaining eggs with the rest of the milk. Remove the dish from the oven and lower the temperature to 150°C/300°F/Gas 2. Break up the meat using two forks and pour over the beaten egg mixture.

6 Scatter the almonds over the top and return to the oven to bake, uncovered, for 30 minutes until set and golden brown all over.

Piquant Chicken with Spaghetti

Serves 4

INGREDIENTS

1 onion, finely chopped
1 carrot, diced
1 garlic clove, crushed
300 ml/½ pint/1¼ cups vegetable
    stock or water
4 small chicken breasts, boned
    and skinned
bouquet garni (bay leaf, parsley
    stalks and thyme)
115 g/4 oz button mushrooms,
    sliced thinly
5 ml/1 tsp wine vinegar or
    lemon juice
350 g/12 oz spaghetti
½ cucumber, peeled and cut
    into fingers
2 firm ripe tomatoes, skinned,
    seeded and chopped
30 ml/2 tbsp low-fat crème fraîche
15 ml/1 tbsp chopped fresh parsley
15 ml/1 tbsp snipped chives
salt and ground black pepper

carrot

chicken breasts   *tomatoes*

cucumber
chives

spaghetti
parsley
thyme

button
mushrooms
bay leaf

vegetable stock   *onion*

1 Put the onion, carrot, garlic, stock or water into a saucepan with the chicken breasts and bouquet garni. Bring to the boil, cover and simmer gently for 15–20 minutes or until tender. Transfer the chicken to a plate and cover with foil.

2 Remove the chicken and strain the liquid. Discard the vegetables and return the liquid to the pan. Add the sliced mushrooms, wine vinegar or lemon juice and simmer for 2–3 minutes until tender.

3 Cook the spaghetti in a large pan of boiling, salted water until *al dente*. Drain thoroughly.

4 Blanch the cucumber in boiling water for 10 seconds. Drain and rinse under cold water.

5 Cut the chicken breasts into bite-size pieces. Boil the stock to reduce by half, then add the chicken, tomatoes, crème fraîche, cucumber and herbs. Season with salt and pepper to taste.

6 Transfer the spaghetti to a warmed serving dish and spoon over the piquant chicken. Serve at once.

NUTRITIONAL NOTES

PER PORTION:

ENERGY 472 Kcals/1981 KJ **FAT** 7.6 g
SATURATED FAT 2.5 g
CHOLESTEROL 65 mg

Chicken and Bean Risotto

Rice, beans, sweetcorn and broccoli add fibre to this healthy chicken dish.

Serves 4–6

INGREDIENTS
1 onion, chopped
2 garlic cloves, crushed
1 fresh red chilli, finely chopped
175 g/6 oz/2¼ cups
  mushrooms, sliced
2 celery sticks, chopped
225 g/8 oz/1 cup long grain
  brown rice
450 ml/¾ pint/1⅞ cups
  chicken stock
150 ml/¼ pint/⅔ cup white wine
225 g/8 oz cooked skinless chicken
  breast, diced
400 g/14 oz can red kidney beans
200 g/7 oz can sweetcorn kernels
115 g/4 oz/⅔ cup sultanas
175 g/6 oz small broccoli florets
30–45 ml/2–3 tbsp chopped fresh
  mixed herbs
salt and ground black pepper

garlic *red chilli*
onion

celery
long grain brown rice
mushrooms

chicken stock *dry white wine*
chicken breasts

red kidney beans

sweetcorn *sultanas* *broccoli*

fresh mixed herbs

1 Put the onion, garlic, chilli, mushrooms, celery, rice, stock and wine in a saucepan. Cover, bring to the boil and simmer for 25 minutes.

2 Stir in the chicken, kidney beans, sweetcorn and sultanas. Cook for a further 10 minutes, until almost all the liquid has been absorbed.

NUTRITIONAL NOTES
Per portion:

ENERGY 353 Kcals/1482 KJ **FAT** 4.2 g
SATURATED FAT 1.1 g
CHOLESTEROL 28.5 mg

3 Meanwhile, cook the broccoli in boiling water for 5 minutes, then drain thoroughly.

4 Stir in the broccoli and chopped herbs, season to taste and serve immediately.

COOK'S TIP
Use 5 ml/1 tsp hot chilli powder in place of the fresh chilli.

Chilli Chicken Couscous

Don't neglect couscous. It provides one of the tastiest ways of adding bulk to a low-fat dish.

Serves 4

INGREDIENTS

225 g/8 oz/2 cups couscous
1 litre/1¾ pints/4 cups boiling water
5 ml/1 tsp olive oil
400 g/14 oz boned and skinned
   chicken portions, diced
1 yellow pepper, seeded and sliced
2 large courgettes, thickly sliced
1 small fresh green chilli, thinly
   sliced, or 5 ml/1 tsp chilli sauce
1 large tomato, diced
425 g/15 oz can chick-peas, drained
salt and ground black pepper
fresh coriander leaves or parsley
   sprigs, to garnish

1 Place the couscous in a large bowl and pour over the boiling water. Cover and leave to stand for 30 minutes.

chicken

olive oil

tomato

yellow pepper

couscous

chick-peas

coriander

green chilli

courgette

NUTRITIONAL NOTES
PER PORTION:

ENERGY 363 Kcals/1525 KJ **FAT** 8.1 g
SATURATED FAT 1.7 g
CHOLESTEROL 57 mg

2 Heat the oil in a non-stick pan. Stir-fry the chicken quickly, then reduce the heat. Stir in the pepper, courgettes and chilli or sauce. Cook for 10 minutes, until the vegetables are softened.

3 Stir in the tomato and chick-peas, then add the couscous. Adjust the seasoning and stir over a medium heat until hot. Serve garnished with fresh coriander leaves or parsley sprigs.

Spicy Chicken and Rice

This dish is a complete meal on its own, but is also delicious served with a lentil dish such as Tarka Dhal.

Serves 4

INGREDIENTS

400 g/14 oz/2 cups basmati rice
30 ml/2 tbsp olive oil
1 onion, sliced
1.5 ml/¼ tsp mixed onion and
    mustard seeds
3 curry leaves
5 ml/1 tsp grated fresh root ginger
1 clove garlic, crushed
5 ml/1 tsp ground coriander
5 ml/1 tsp chilli powder
7.5 ml/1½ tsp salt
2 tomatoes, sliced
1 potato, cubed
50 g/2 oz/½ cup frozen peas
175 g/6 oz boned and skinned
    chicken breast, cubed
60 ml/4 tbsp chopped fresh
    coriander
2 fresh green chillies, chopped
750 ml/1¼ pints/3 cups water

1 Rinse the rice in several changes of cold water, then soak in fresh cold water for 30 minutes. Drain and set aside. In a non-stick saucepan, heat the oil and fry the sliced onion until golden.

2 Add the onion and mustard seeds, the curry leaves, ginger, garlic, ground coriander, chilli powder and salt. Stir-fry for about 2 minutes.

3 Add the sliced tomatoes, cubed potato, thawed peas and cubed chicken and mix well.

4 Add the rice and stir gently to combine with the other ingredients.

chicken

mustard seeds

curry leaves

ginger

frozen peas

onion

olive oil

tomatoes

potato

garlic

ground coriander

chilli powder

green chillies

fresh coriander

basmati rice

5 Finally, add the fresh coriander and chopped green chillies. Mix well. Toss over the heat for 1 minute more. Pour in the water. Bring to the boil and reduce the heat to the lowest setting. Cover and cook for about 20 minutes, by which time all the liquid should have been absorbed and the mixture should be fragrant. Serve at once.

NUTRITIONAL NOTES

PER PORTION:

ENERGY 406 Kcals/1707 KJ **FAT** 8.5 g
SATURATED FAT 1.9 g
CHOLESTEROL 25.1 mg

Chicken Kebabs and Rice

This marinade contains sugar and will burn very easily, so grill the kebabs slowly, turning often. Serve with Harlequin Rice.

Serves 4

INGREDIENTS
2 boned and skinned chicken breasts
8 pickling onions or 2 medium
   onions, peeled
4 rindless streaky bacon rashers
3 firm bananas
1 red pepper, seeded and diced

FOR THE MARINADE
30 ml/2 tbsp soft brown sugar
15 ml/1 tbsp Worcestershire sauce
30 ml/2 tbsp lemon juice
salt and freshly ground black pepper

FOR THE HARLEQUIN RICE
30 ml/2 tbsp olive oil
225 g/8 oz/generous 1 cup
   cooked rice
115 g/4 oz/1 cup cooked peas
1 small red pepper, seeded and diced

pepper

Worcestershire
sauce

lemon

bacon

sugar

onions

bananas

chicken breast

1 Mix together the marinade ingredients. Cut each chicken breast into four pieces, add to the marinade, cover and leave for at least four hours or preferably overnight.

2 Peel the pickling onions, blanch them in boiling water for 5 minutes and drain. If using medium onions, quarter them after blanching.

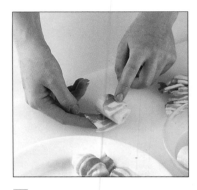

3 Cut each rasher of bacon in half. Peel the bananas and cut each into three pieces. Wrap a rasher of bacon around each piece of banana.

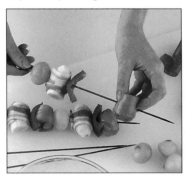

4 Thread onto metal skewers with the chicken pieces, onions and pepper pieces. Brush with the marinade.

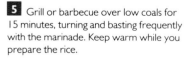

5 Grill or barbecue over low coals for 15 minutes, turning and basting frequently with the marinade. Keep warm while you prepare the rice.

COOK'S TIP

Pour boiling water over the small onions and then drain, to make peeling easier.

6 Heat the oil in a frying pan and add the rice, peas and diced pepper. Stir until heated through and serve with the kebabs.

Chicken and Rice Stir-fry

This dish is originally from Thailand, but can easily be adapted by adding any cooked ingredients you have to hand. Crispy prawn crackers make an ideal accompaniment.

NUTRITIONAL NOTES
PER PORTION:

ENERGY 423 Kcals/1778 KJ **FAT** 10.4 g
SATURATED FAT 2.3 g
CHOLESTEROL 184.6 mg

Serves 4

INGREDIENTS
225 g/8 oz long grain rice
2 × size 3 eggs
30 ml/2 tbsp vegetable oil
1 green chilli
2 spring onions, roughly chopped
2 cloves garlic, crushed
225 g/8 oz cooked chicken
225 g/8 oz cooked prawns
45 ml/3 tbsp dark soy sauce
prawn crackers, to serve

rice

soy sauce

egg

chilli

prawns

1 Rinse the rice and then cook for 10–12 minutes in 500 ml/1 pint water in a saucepan with a tight-fitting lid. When cooked, refresh under cold water.

2 Lightly beat the eggs. Heat 15 ml/1 tbsp of oil in a small frying pan and swirl in the beaten egg. When cooked on one side, flip over and cook on the other side, remove from the pan and leave to cool. Cut the omelette into strips.

3 Carefully remove the seeds from the chilli and chop finely, wearing rubber gloves to protect your hands if necessary. Place the spring onions, chilli and garlic in a food processor and blend to a paste.

4 Heat the wok, and then add the remaining oil. When the oil is hot, add the paste and stir-fry for 1 minute.

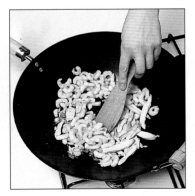

5 Add the chicken and prawns.

6 Add the rice and stir-fry for 3–4 minutes. Stir in the soy sauce and serve with prawn crackers.

Caribbean Chicken Kebabs

These kebabs have a rich, robust flavour and the marinade keeps them moist without the need for oil. Serve with a colourful salad and rice.

Serves 4

INGREDIENTS
500 g/1¼ lb boned and skinned
  chicken breasts
finely grated rind of 1 lime
30 ml/2 tbsp fresh lime juice
15 ml/1 tbsp rum or sherry
15 ml/1 tbsp light muscovado sugar
5 ml/1 tsp ground cinnamon
2 mangoes, peeled and cubed

chicken

lime

rum

*light
muscovado
sugar*

*ground
cinnamon*

mango

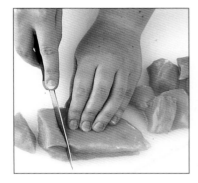

1 Cut the chicken into bite-size chunks and place in a bowl with the lime rind and juice, rum or sherry, sugar and cinnamon. Toss well, cover and leave to stand for 1 hour.

2 Drain the chicken, saving the juices and thread on to four wooden skewers, alternating with the mango cubes.

3 Grill the skewers or cook on a hot barbecue for 8–10 minutes, turning occasionally and basting with the juices, until the chicken is tender and golden brown. Serve at once with rice and salad.

COOK'S TIP

Soak the skewers in cold water for 30 minutes before filling them. This prevents the wood from scorching.

NUTRITIONAL NOTES

PER PORTION:

ENERGY 218 Kcals/918 KJ **FAT** 4.2 g
SATURATED FAT 1.3 g
CHOLESTEROL 53.8 mg

Chicken Fried Noodles

This delicious dish makes a filling meal. Take care when frying vermicelli as it has a tendency to spit when added to hot oil.

Serves 4

INGREDIENTS
125 ml/4 fl oz/½ cup vegetable oil
225 g/8 oz rice vermicelli
150 g/5 oz French beans, topped, tailed and halved lengthwise
1 onion, finely chopped
2 boneless, skinless chicken breasts, about 175 g/6 oz each, cut into strips
5 ml/1 tsp chilli powder
225 g/8 oz cooked prawns
45 ml/3 tbsp dark soy sauce
45 ml/3 tbsp white wine vinegar
10 ml/2 tsp caster sugar
fresh coriander sprigs, to garnish

rice vermicelli

chicken breast

onion

French beans

prawns

NUTRITIONAL NOTES
PER PORTION:

ENERGY 487 Kcals/2045 KJ **FAT** 15 g
SATURATED FAT 2.6 g
CHOLESTEROL 83.2 mg

1 Heat the wok, then add 60 ml/4 tbsp of the oil. Break up the vermicelli into 7.5 cm/3 in lengths. When the oil is hot, fry the vermicelli in batches. Remove from the heat and keep warm.

2 Heat the remaining oil in the wok, then add the French beans, onion and chicken and stir-fry for 3 minutes until the chicken is cooked.

3 Sprinkle in the chilli powder. Stir in the prawns, soy sauce, vinegar and sugar, and stir-fry for 2 minutes.

4 Serve the chicken, prawns and vegetables on the vermicelli, garnished with sprigs of fresh coriander.

Tortellini

Serves 6–8 as a starter or 4–6 as a main course

INGREDIENTS

115 g/4oz smoked, lean ham
115 g/4 oz chicken breast, boned
   and skinned
900 ml/1½ pint/3¾ cups chicken or
   vegetable stock
coriander stalks
30 ml/2 tbsp grated Parmesan
   cheese, plus extra for serving
1 egg, beaten, plus egg white
   for brushing
30 ml/2 tbsp chopped
   fresh coriander
1 quantity of basic pasta dough
flour, for dusting
salt and ground black pepper
coriander leaves, to garnish

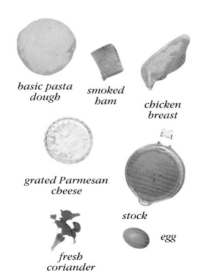

basic pasta dough *smoked ham* *chicken breast*

grated Parmesan cheese

stock

egg

fresh coriander

1 Cut the ham and chicken into large chunks and put them into a saucepan with 150 ml/¼ pint/⅔ cup of the chicken or vegetable stock and some coriander stalks. Bring to the boil, cover and simmer for 20 minutes until tender. Cool slightly in the stock.

2 Drain the ham and chicken and mince finely (reserve the stock). Put into a bowl with the Parmesan cheese, beaten egg, chopped coriander and season with salt and pepper.

3 Roll the pasta into thin sheets, cut into 4 cm/1½ in squares. Put 2.5 ml/½ tsp of filling on each. Brush edges with egg white and fold each square into a triangle; press out any air and seal firmly.

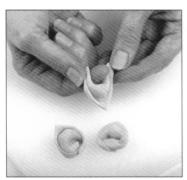

4 Curl each triangle around the tip of a forefinger and press the two ends together firmly.

5 Lay on a lightly floured tea towel to rest for 30 minutes before cooking.

NUTRITIONAL NOTES
PER PORTION:

ENERGY 335 Kcals/1405 KJ **FAT** 9.7 g
SATURATED FAT 3.6 g
CHOLESTEROL 193 mg

6 Strain the reserved stock and add to the remainder. Put into a pan and bring to the boil. Lower the heat to a gentle boil and add the tortellini. Cook for 5 minutes. Then turn off the heat, cover the pan and stand for 20–30 minutes. Serve in soup plates with some of the stock, garnish with coriander leaves. Serve grated Parmesan separately.

Chicken Kiev

Cut through the crispy-coated chicken to reveal a creamy filling with just a hint of garlic.

Serves 4

INGREDIENTS
4 large chicken breasts, boned and skinned
15 ml/1 tbsp lemon juice
115 g/4 oz/½ cup ricotta cheese
1 garlic clove, crushed
30 ml/2 tbsp chopped fresh parsley
¼ tsp freshly grated nutmeg
30 ml/2 tbsp plain flour
pinch of cayenne pepper
¼ tsp salt
115 g/4 oz/2 cups fresh white breadcrumbs
2 egg whites, lightly beaten
duchesse potatoes, French beans and grilled tomatoes, to serve

breadcrumbs

egg whites

chicken breast

ricotta cheese

garlic

parsley

1 Pre-heat the oven to 200°C/400°F/Gas 6. Place the chicken breasts between two sheets of clear film and gently beat with a rolling pin until flattened. Sprinkle with the lemon juice.

2 Mix the ricotta cheese with the garlic, 15 ml/1 tbsp of the chopped parsley, and the nutmeg. Shape into four 5-cm/2-in long cylinders.

3 Put one portion of the cheese and herb mixture in the centre of each chicken breast and fold the meat over, tucking in the edges to enclose the filling completely.

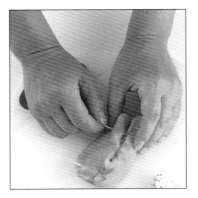

4 Secure the chicken with cocktail sticks pushed through the centre of each. Mix together the flour, cayenne pepper and salt. Dust the chicken with the seasoned flour.

5 Mix together the breadcrumbs and remaining parsley. Dip the chicken into the egg whites, then coat with the breadcrumbs. Chill for 30 minutes in the refrigerator, then dip into the egg white and breadcrumbs for a second time.

NUTRITIONAL NOTES
Per portion:

ENERGY 354.5 Kcals/1489 KJ **FAT** 9.0 g
SATURATED FAT 3.5 g
CHOLESTEROL 78.9 mg

6 Put the chicken on a non-stick baking sheet and spray with non-stick cooking spray. Bake in the pre-heated oven for 25 minutes or until the coating is golden brown and the chicken completely cooked. Remove the cocktail sticks and serve with duchesse potatoes, French beans and grilled tomatoes.

Minty Yogurt Chicken

Honey, lime juice and fresh mint make a
marvellous marinade.

Serves 4

INGREDIENTS
8 chicken thigh portions, skinned
15 ml/1 tbsp clear honey
30 ml/2 tbsp lime juice
30 ml/2 tbsp low fat natural yogurt
60 ml/4 tbsp chopped fresh mint
salt and ground black pepper

chicken thighs

honey

lime juice

natural yogurt

mint

1 Slash the chicken flesh at intervals
with a sharp knife. Place in a bowl.

2 Mix the honey, lime juice, yogurt and
half the mint in a bowl. Add salt and
pepper to taste.

3 Spoon the marinade over the
chicken. Cover and set aside for
30 minutes.

4 Line a grill pan with foil and cook the
chicken under a moderately hot grill until
thoroughly cooked and golden brown,
turning the portions occasionally during
cooking. Sprinkle with remaining mint,
and serve. Potatoes and a tomato salad
are all you need as accompaniments.

NUTRITIONAL NOTES
PER PORTION:

ENERGY 171 Kcals/719KJ **FAT** 6.7 g
SATURATED FAT 2.2 g
CHOLESTEROL 97.9 mg

Chicken in Creamy Orange Sauce

This sauce is deceptively creamy – in fact it is made with low fat fromage frais, which is virtually fat-free. The brandy adds a richer flavour, but is optional – omit it if you prefer and use orange juice on its own.

Serves 4

INGREDIENTS
8 skinned chicken thighs or
  drumsticks
45 ml/3 tbsp brandy
300 ml/½ pint/1¼ cups orange juice
3 spring onions, chopped
10 ml/2 tsp cornflour
90 ml/6 tbsp low fat fromage frais
salt and ground black pepper

chicken thighs

brandy

spring onions

cornflour

fromage frais

1 Fry the chicken pieces without fat in a non-stick frying pan, turning until evenly browned.

2 Stir in the brandy, orange juice and spring onions. Bring to the boil, then cover and simmer for 15 minutes, or until the chicken is tender and the juices run clear, not pink, when pierced.

3 Blend the cornflour with a little water then mix into the fromage frais. Stir this into the sauce and stir over a medium heat until thickened.

4 Adjust the seasoning and serve with boiled rice or pasta and green salad.

NUTRITIONAL NOTES
PER PORTION:

ENERGY 227 Kcals/951 KJ **FAT** 6.8 g
SATURATED FAT 2.2 g
CHOLESTEROL 87.8 mg

Chicken and Pineapple Kebabs

This chicken has a delicate tang and is very tender. The pineapple gives a slight sweetness to the chicken.

Serves 6

INGREDIENTS

227 g/8 oz can pineapple chunks in natural juice
5 ml/1 tsp ground cumin
5 ml/1 tsp ground coriander
1 small garlic clove, crushed
5 ml/1 tsp chilli powder
5 ml/1 tsp salt
30 ml/2 tbsp low fat natural yogurt
15 ml/1 tbsp chopped fresh coriander
few drops of orange food colouring (optional)
275 g/10 oz skinned and boned chicken breasts
½ red pepper
½ yellow or green pepper
1 large onion
9 cherry tomatoes
10 ml/2 tsp corn oil

chicken

ground cumin

chilli powder

garlic

ground coriander

natural yogurt

fresh coriander

pineapple

red pepper

yellow pepper

onion

cherry tomatoes

corn oil

1 Drain the pineapple juice into a bowl. Reserve 12 large chunks of pineapple and squeeze the juice from the remaining chunks into the bowl and set aside. You should have about 120 ml/4 fl oz/½ cup of pineapple juice. Make up with water if necessary.

2 In a large mixing bowl, combine the ground cumin, ground coriander, garlic, chilli powder, salt, yogurt, fresh coriander and food colouring, if using. Pour in the reserved pineapple juice and mix well.

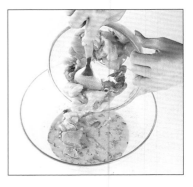

3 Cut the chicken into bite-size cubes, add to the yogurt and spice mixture, cover and leave to marinate for 1–1½ hours. Meanwhile cut the peppers and onion into bite-size chunks.

4 Preheat the grill to medium. Drain the chicken pieces, reserving the marinade, and thread on to six wooden or metal skewers, alternating with the vegetables and reserved pineapple chunks.

5 Brush the kebabs with the oil, then place the skewers on a flameproof dish or in a grill pan. Grill, turning and basting the chicken pieces with the marinade regularly, for about 15 minutes, or until the chicken is cooked. Serve with salad or plain boiled rice.

NUTRITIONAL NOTES

Per portion:

ENERGY 170 Kcals/716 KJ **FAT** 6.7 g
SATURATED FAT 1.5 g
CHOLESTEROL 40.6 mg

Chicken with Orange and Mustard Sauce

The beauty of this recipe is its simplicity; the chicken continues to cook in its own juices while you prepare the sauce.

Serves 4

INGREDIENTS
2 large oranges
4 chicken breasts, boned and skinned
5 ml/1 tsp sunflower oil
salt and freshly ground black pepper
new potatoes and sliced courgettes
    tossed in parsley, to serve

FOR THE ORANGE AND MUSTARD SAUCE
10 ml/2 tsp cornflour
150 ml/¼ pint/⅔ cup strained yogurt
5 ml/1 tsp Dijon mustard

chicken breast

yogurt

cornflour

mustard

orange

NUTRITIONAL NOTES
PER PORTION:

ENERGY 215 Kcals/906 KJ **FAT** 5.4 g
SATURATED FAT 1.7 g
CHOLESTEROL 55.3 mg

1 Peel the oranges using a sharp knife, removing all the white pith. Remove the segments by cutting between the membranes, holding the fruit over a small bowl to catch any juice. Set aside with the juice until required.

2 Season the chicken with salt and freshly ground black pepper. Heat the oil in a non-stick frying pan and cook the chicken for 5 minutes on each side. Take out of the frying pan and wrap in foil; the meat will continue to cook for a while.

3 For the sauce, blend together the cornflour with the juice from the orange. Add the yogurt and mustard. Put into the frying pan and slowly bring to the boil. Simmer for 1 minute.

4 Add the orange segments to the sauce and heat gently. Unwrap the chicken and add any excess juices to the sauce. Slice on the diagonal and serve with the sauce, new potatoes and sliced courgettes tossed in parsley.

Moroccan Spiced Roast Poussins

The combination of dried fruit and spices is typical of North African cooking.

Serves 4

INGREDIENTS

115 g/4 oz/1 cup cooked long
grain rice, plus extra for serving
1 small onion, finely chopped
finely grated rind and juice of
1 lemon
30 ml/2 tbsp chopped fresh mint
45 ml/3 tbsp chopped ready-to-eat
dried apricots
30 ml/2 tbsp natural low fat yogurt
10 ml/2 tsp ground turmeric
10 ml/2 tsp ground cumin
2 poussins, each about 450g/1 lb
salt and ground black pepper
lemon slices and fresh mint sprigs,
to garnish

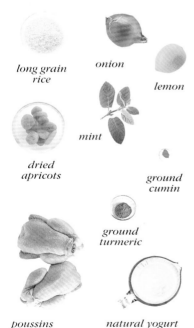

long grain rice

onion

lemon

mint

dried apricots

ground cumin

ground turmeric

poussins

natural yogurt

1 Preheat the oven to 200°C/400°F/ Gas 6. Mix the rice, onion, lemon rind, mint and apricots in a bowl. Stir in half each of the lemon juice, yogurt, turmeric and cumin. Season with salt and pepper.

2 Stuff the neck of the poussins with the rice. Place the poussins on a rack in a roasting tin.

NUTRITIONAL NOTES
PER PORTION:

ENERGY 219 Kcals/919 KJ **FAT** 6.0 g
SATURATED FAT 1.9 g
CHOLESTEROL 71.6 mg

3 Mix together the remaining lemon juice, yogurt, turmeric and cumin, then brush this over the poussins. Cover loosely with foil and roast for 30 minutes.

4 Remove the foil and roast for a further 15 minutes, or until the birds are golden brown and the juices run clear, not pink, when pierced.

5 Cut the poussins in half with a sharp knife or poultry shears, and serve with cooked rice, if you like. Garnish with lemon and fresh mint.

Chicken with Green Mango

Green, unripe mango is used for making various Indian dishes, including this simple chicken dish.

NUTRITIONAL NOTES
Per portion:

ENERGY 269 Kcals/1131 KJ **FAT** 11.0 g
SATURATED FAT 2.4 g
CHOLESTEROL 64.1 mg

Serves 4

INGREDIENTS
1 medium green (unripe) mango
450 g/1 lb boned and skinned
  chicken breasts, cubed
1.5 ml/¼ tsp onion seeds
5 ml/1 tsp grated fresh root ginger
1 small garlic clove, crushed
5 ml/1 tsp chilli powder
1.5 ml/¼ tsp turmeric
5 ml/1 tsp salt
5 ml/1 tsp ground coriander
30 ml/2 tbsp corn oil
2 onions, sliced
4 curry leaves
300 ml/½ pint/1¼ cups water
2 tomatoes, quartered
2 fresh green chillies, chopped
30 ml/2 tbsp fresh coriander

1 Peel the mango and slice the flesh thickly. Discard the stone. Place the mango slices in a small bowl, cover and set aside.

2 Place the chicken cubes in a bowl and add the onion seeds, ginger, garlic, chilli powder, turmeric, salt and ground coriander. Mix the spices into the chicken and add half the mango slices to this mixture as well.

3 In a medium saucepan, heat the oil and fry the sliced onions until golden brown. Add the curry leaves.

chicken

turmeric

ginger

onion seeds

garlic

chilli powder

green mango

corn oil

fresh coriander

4 Gradually add the spiced chicken cubes, stirring all the time.

onion

ground coriander

curry leaves

tomatoes

green chillies

5 Pour in the water, bring to the boil, then lower the heat and cook for 12–15 minutes, stirring occasionally, until the chicken is cooked through and the water has evaporated.

6 Add the remaining mango slices, the tomatoes, green chillies and fresh coriander. Mix lightly and serve.

Chicken Roll

The roll can be prepared and cooked the day before and will freeze well too. Remove from the refrigerator about an hour before serving.

Serves 8

INGREDIENTS
1 × 2 kg/4 lb chicken

FOR THE STUFFING
1 medium onion, finely chopped
50 g/2 oz/4 tbsp melted butter
350 g/12 oz lean minced pork
115 g/4 oz streaky bacon, chopped
15 ml/1 tbsp chopped fresh parsley
10 ml/2 tsp chopped fresh thyme
115 g/4 oz/2 cups fresh white
   breadcrumbs
30 ml/2 tbsp sherry
1 large egg, beaten
25 g/1 oz/¼ cup shelled pistachio
   nuts
25 g/1 oz/¼ cup stoned black olives
   (about 12)
salt and freshly ground black pepper

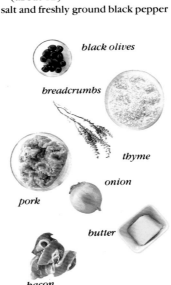

black olives

breadcrumbs

thyme

onion

pork

butter

bacon

1 To make the stuffing, cook the chopped onion gently in 25 g/1 oz/2 tbsp butter until soft. Turn into a bowl and cool. Add the remaining ingredients, mix thoroughly and season with salt and freshly ground black pepper.

2 To bone the chicken, use a small, sharp knife to remove the wing tips (pinions). Turn the chicken onto its breast and cut a line down the back bone.

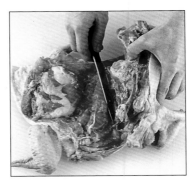

3 Cut the flesh away from the carcass, scraping the bones clean. Carefully cut through the sinew around the leg and wing joints and scrape down the bones to free them. Remove the carcass, taking care not to cut through the skin along the breast bone.

4 To stuff the chicken, lay it flat, skin side down and level the flesh as much as possible. Shape the stuffing down the centre of the chicken and fold the sides over the stuffing.

5 Sew the flesh neatly together, using a needle and dark thread. Tie with fine string into a roll.

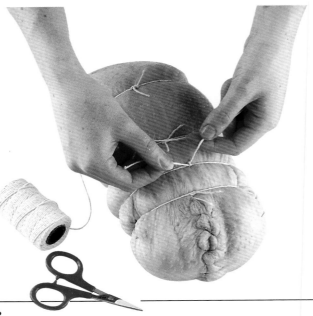

COOK'S TIPS

Thaw the chicken roll from frozen for 12 hours in the refrigerator, and leave to stand at cool room temperature for an hour before serving.

Use dark thread for sewing, as it is much easier to see so that you can remove it once the roll is cooked.

NUTRITIONAL NOTES

Per portion:

ENERGY 235 Kcals/990 KJ **FAT** 14.9 g
SATURATED FAT 4.4 g
CHOLESTEROL 99.7 mg

6 Preheat the oven to 180°C/350°F/Gas 4. Place the roll, with the join underneath, on a roasting rack in a roasting tin and brush generously with the remaining butter. Bake uncovered for about 1¼ hours or until cooked. Baste the chicken often with the juices in the roasting tin. Leave to cool completely before removing the string and thread. Wrap in foil and chill until ready for serving or freezing.

Chilli Chicken

Serve as a simple supper dish with boiled potatoes and broccoli, or as a party dish with rice.

Serves 4

INGREDIENTS
12 chicken thighs
15 ml/1 tbsp olive oil
1 medium onion, thinly sliced
1 garlic clove, crushed
5 ml/1 tsp chilli powder or 1 fresh
  chilli, chopped
1 × 400 g/14 oz can chopped
  tomatoes, with their juice
5 ml/1 tsp caster sugar
1 × 425 g/15 oz can red kidney beans,
  drained
salt and freshly ground black pepper

red kidney beans

tomatoes

onion

olive oil

garlic

chicken thighs

caster sugar

chilli powder

1 Cut the chicken into large cubes, removing all skin and bones. Heat the oil in a large flameproof casserole and brown the chicken pieces on all sides. Remove and keep warm.

2 Add the onion and garlic clove to the casserole and cook until tender. Add the chilli powder or fresh chilli and cook for 2 minutes. Add the tomatoes with their juice, seasoning and sugar.

NUTRITIONAL NOTES
PER PORTION:

ENERGY 352 Kcals/1479 KJ **FAT** 13.4 g
SATURATED FAT 3.8 g
CHOLESTEROL 131.4 mg

3 Replace the chicken pieces, cover the casserole and simmer for about 30 minutes until tender.

4 Add the red kidney beans and gently cook for a further 5 minutes to heat them through before serving.

Citrus Kebabs

Serve on a bed of lettuce leaves and garnish with fresh mint and orange and lemon slices.

Serves 4

INGREDIENTS
4 chicken breasts, skinned and boned
fresh mint sprigs, to garnish
orange, lemon or lime slices, to
    garnish (optional)

FOR THE MARINADE
finely grated rind and juice of
    ½ orange
finely grated rind and juice of ½ small
    lemon or lime
30 ml/2 tbsp olive oil
30 ml/2 tbsp clear honey
30 ml/2 tbsp chopped fresh mint
1.25 ml/¼ tsp ground cumin
salt and freshly ground black pepper

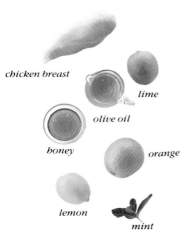

chicken breast

lime

olive oil

honey   *orange*

lemon

mint

NUTRITIONAL NOTES
PER PORTION:

ENERGY 229 Kcals/960 KJ **FAT** 9.6 g
SATURATED FAT 2.10 g
CHOLESTEROL 53.8 mg

1 Cut the chicken into cubes of approximately 2.5 cm/1 in.

2 Mix the marinade ingredients together, add the chicken cubes and leave to marinate for at least 2 hours.

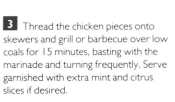

3 Thread the chicken pieces onto skewers and grill or barbecue over low coals for 15 minutes, basting with the marinade and turning frequently. Serve garnished with extra mint and citrus slices if desired.

Tagine of Chicken

Based on a traditional Moroccan dish. The chicken and couscous can be cooked the day before and reheated for serving.

Serves 8

INGREDIENTS
8 chicken legs (thighs and drumsticks)
30 ml/2 tbsp olive oil
1 medium onion, finely chopped
2 garlic cloves, crushed
5 ml/1 tsp ground turmeric
2.5 ml/½ tsp ground ginger
2.5 ml/½ tsp ground cinnamon
450 ml/¾ pint/1⅞ cups chicken
   stock
150 g/5 oz/1¼ cups stoned green
   olives
1 lemon, sliced
salt and freshly ground black pepper
fresh coriander sprigs, to garnish

FOR THE VEGETABLE COUSCOUS
600 ml/1 pint/2½ cups chicken stock
450 g/1 lb couscous
4 courgettes, thickly sliced
2 carrots, thickly sliced
2 small turnips, peeled and cubed
45 ml/3 tbsp olive oil
1 × 450 g/15 oz can chick peas,
   drained

1 Preheat the oven to 180°C/350°F/ Gas 4. Cut the chicken legs into two through the joint.

2 Heat the oil in a large flameproof casserole and working in batches, brown the chicken on both sides. Remove and keep warm.

3 Add the onion and crushed garlic to the flameproof casserole and cook gently until tender. Add the spices and cook for 1 minute. Pour over the stock, bring to the boil, and return the chicken. Cover and bake for 45 minutes until tender.

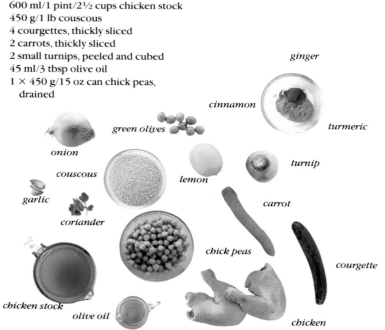

ginger

cinnamon

green olives

turmeric

onion

couscous

turnip

lemon

garlic

coriander

carrot

chick peas

courgette

chicken stock

olive oil

chicken

4 Transfer the chicken to a bowl, cover and keep warm. Remove any fat from the cooking liquid and boil to reduce by one-third. Meanwhile, blanch the olives and lemon slices in a pan of boiling water for 2 minutes until the lemon skin is tender. Drain and add to the cooking liquid, adjusting the seasoning to taste.

5 To cook the couscous, bring the stock to the boil in a large pan and sprinkle in the couscous slowly, stirring all the time. Remove from the heat, cover and leave to stand for 5 minutes.

COOK'S TIP
The couscous can be reheated with
30 ml/2 tbsp olive oil in a steamer
over a pan of boiling water, stirring
occasionally. If you cook the chicken
in advance, undercook the chicken by
15 minutes and reheat in the oven for
20–30 minutes.

NUTRITIONAL NOTES
Per portion:

ENERGY 350 Kcals/1470 KJ **FAT** 10.8 g
SATURATED FAT 2.3 g
CHOLESTEROL 65.7 mg

6 Meanwhile, cook the vegetables,
drain and put them into a large bowl. Add
the couscous and oil and season. Stir the
grains to fluff them up, add the chick peas
and finally the chopped coriander. Spoon
onto a large serving plate, cover with the
chicken pieces, and spoon over the liquid.
Garnish with fresh coriander sprigs.

Chicken with Prawns

For this extra-special party dish, the skin is left on the chicken for extra flavour, but the general fat content is reduced by low fat cooking techniques.

Serves 4

INGREDIENTS

1 chicken, about 1.5 kg/3–3½ lb, cut
  into 8 pieces
10 ml/2 tsp corn oil
12 large raw prawns or live crayfish,
  with heads if possible
1 small onion, halved and sliced
30 ml/2 tbsp plain flour
175 ml/6 fl oz/¾ cup dry white wine
30 ml/2 tbsp brandy
300 ml/½ pint/1¼ cups defatted
  chicken stock
3 tomatoes, cored and quartered
1 or 2 garlic cloves, finely chopped
bouquet garni
60 ml/4 tbsp reduced-fat
  whipping cream
salt and ground black pepper
fresh parsley, to garnish

COOK'S TIP

To prepare ahead, cook as directed up to step 5. Cool and chill the chicken and sauce. To serve, reheat the chicken and sauce over a medium-low heat for about 30 minutes. Add the prawn or crayfish tails and heat through.

1 Wash the chicken pieces, then pat dry with kitchen paper and season with salt and pepper. Heat the oil in a large flameproof casserole and cook the prawns or crayfish over a high heat until they turn a bright colour. Remove the prawns or crayfish, cool slightly and then peel away the heads and shells and reserve. Chill the peeled tails.

2 Add the chicken to the casserole, skin side down, and cook over a medium-high heat for 10–12 minutes until golden brown, turning to colour evenly and cooking in batches if necessary. Transfer the chicken to a plate and pour off all but 15 ml/1 tbsp of the fat.

3 In the same casserole, cook the onion over a medium-high heat until golden, stirring frequently. Sprinkle with flour and continue cooking for 2 minutes, stirring frequently, then add the wine and brandy and bring to the boil, stirring constantly.

chicken

corn oil

plain flour

garlic

large prawns

white wine

brandy

small onion

tomatoes

chicken stock

bouquet garni

whipping cream

NUTRITIONAL NOTES

PER PORTION:

ENERGY 446 Kcals/1873 KJ **FAT** 13.0 g
SATURATED FAT 4.4 g
CHOLESTEROL 292 mg

4 Add the stock, prawn or crayfish heads and shells, tomatoes, garlic and bouquet garni with the chicken pieces and any juices. Bring to the boil, then cover the casserole and simmer for 20–25 minutes until the chicken is tender and the juices run clear when the thickest part of the meat is pierced.

5 Remove the chicken pieces from the casserole and strain the cooking liquid, pressing down on the shells and vegetables to extract as much liquid as possible. Skim off the fat from the cooking liquid and return the liquid to the pan. Add the cream and boil until it is reduced by one-third and slightly thickened.

6 Return the chicken pieces to the pan and simmer for 5 minutes. Just before serving, add the prawns or crayfish tails and heat through. Arrange on warmed plates. pour over some of the sauce and garnish with fresh parsley.